THE TEMPEST

By WILLIAM SHAKESPEARE

Preface and Annotations by
HENRY N. HUDSON

Introduction by
CHARLES HAROLD HERFORD

Bridge UP 2019

Congratulations!
"Oh Brave New World!"

Rob

The Tempest
By William Shakespeare
Preface and Annotations by Henry N. Hudson
Introduction by Charles Harold Herford

Print ISBN 13: 978-1-4209-5340-4
eBook ISBN 13: 978-1-4209-5341-1

Cover Image: A detail of "Miranda," 1916 (oil on canvas), Waterhouse, John William (1849-1917) / Private Collection / Photo © The Maas Gallery, London / Bridgeman Images.

Please visit *www.digireads.com*

CONTENTS

Preface

First printed in the folio of 1623. The play is badly printed, considerably worse than most of the plays originally printed in that volume; though not so badly as *All's Well*, *Timon of Athens*, and *Coriolanus*. Besides many slighter errors, not very difficult of correction, it has a number of passages that are troublesome in the highest degree, and some that have hitherto baffled the most persevering and painstaking efforts to bring them into a satisfactory state; insomuch that they should, perhaps, be left untouched, as hopelessly incurable. Still I suppose it would hardly do to give up the cause on the plea that the resources of corrective art have here been exhausted. The details of the matter are, I believe, fully presented in the Critical Notes, and therefore need not be further enlarged upon here.

It has been ascertained beyond question that *The Tempest* was written at some time between the years 1603 and 1613. On the one hand, the leading features of Gonzalo's Commonwealth, as described in Act ii., scene 1, were evidently taken from John Florio's translation of Montaigne, which was published in 1603. In Montaigne's essay *Of the Cannibals*, as translated by Florio, we have the following: "Meseemeth that what in these nations we see by experience doth not only exceed all the pictures wherewith licentious Poesy hath proudly embellished the golden age, and all her quaint inventions to feign a happy condition of man, but also the conception and desire of Philosophy. It is a nation, would I answer Plato, that hath no kind of traffic, no knowledge of letters, no intelligence of numbers, no name of magistrate, nor of politic superiority; no use of service, of riches, or of poverty; no contracts, no successions, no dividences; no occupation, but idle; no respect of kindred, but common; no apparel but natural; no manuring of lands; no use of wine, corn, or metal: the very words that import lying, falsehood, treason, dissimulation, covetousness, envy, detraction, and pardon, were never heard amongst them."

Here the borrowing is too plain to be questioned; and this fixes the writing of *The Tempest* after 1603. On the other hand, Malone ascertained from some old records that the play was acted by the King's players "before Prince Charles, the Princess Elizabeth, and the Prince Palatine, in the beginning of 1613."

But the time of writing is to be gathered more nearly from another source. The play has several points clearly connecting with some of the then recent marvels of Transatlantic discovery: in fact, I suspect America may justly claim to have borne a considerable part in suggesting and shaping this delectable workmanship. In May, 1609, Sir George Somers, with a fleet of nine ships, headed by the *Sea-Venture*, which was called the Admiral's Ship, sailed for Virginia. In mid-ocean they were struck by a terrible tempest, which scattered the whole fleet; seven of the ships, however, reached Virginia; but the *Sea-Venture* was parted from the rest, driven out of her course, and finally wrecked on one of the Bermudas. These islands were then thought to be "a most prodigious and enchanted place, affording nothing but gusts, storms, and foul weather"; on which account they had acquired a bad name, as "an enchanted pile of rocks, and a desert inhabitation of devils."

In 1610 appeared a pamphlet entitled *A Discovery of the Bermudas, otherwise called the Isle of Devils*, giving an account of the storm and shipwreck. The sailors had worked themselves into complete exhaustion, had given over in despair, and taken leave of each other, when the ship was found to be jammed in between two rocks, so that all came safe to land. They found the island uninhabited, the air mild and wholesome, the land exceedingly fruitful; "all the fairies of the rocks were but flocks of birds, and all the devils that haunted the woods were but herds of swine." Staying there some nine months, they had a very delightful time of it, refitted their ship, and then put to sea again, with an ample supply of provisions, and their minds richly freighted with the beauties and wonders of the place.

There can be no rational doubt that from this narrative Shakespeare took various hints for the matter of his drama. Thus much is plainly indicated by his mention of "the still-vex'd Bermoothes," as the Bermudas were then called, and also by the qualities of air and soil ascribed to his happy island. So that 1610 is as early a date as can well be assigned for the composition. The supernatural in the play was no doubt the Poet's own creation; but it would have been in accordance with his usual method to avail himself of whatever interest might spring from the popular notions touching the Bermudas. In his marvellous creations the people would see nothing but the distant marvels with which their fancies were prepossessed.

Concurrent with all this is the internal evidence of the play itself. The style, language, and general cast of thought, the union of richness and severity, the grave, austere beauty of character which pervades it, and the organic compactness of the whole structure, all go to mark it as an issue of the Poet's ripest years. Coleridge regarded it as "certainly one of Shakespeare's latest works, judging from the language only." Campbell the poet considers it his very latest. "*The Tempest*," says he, "has a sort of sacredness as the last work of a mighty workman. Shakespeare, as if conscious that it would be his last, and as if inspired to typify himself, has made his hero a natural, a dignified, and benevolent magician, who could conjure up 'spirits from the vasty deep,' and command supernatural agency by the most seemingly-natural and simple means. Shakespeare himself is Prospero, or rather the superior genius who commands both Prospero and Ariel. But the time was approaching when the potent sorcerer was to break his staff, and bury it fathoms in the ocean 'deeper than did ever plummet sound.' That staff has never been and will never be recovered."

But I suspect there is more of poetry than of truth in this; at least I can find no warrant for it: on the contrary, we have fair ground for believing that at least *Coriolanus*, *King Henry the Eighth*, and perhaps *The Winter's Tale* were written after *The Tempest.* Verplanck, rather than give up the notion so well put by Campbell, suggests that the Poet may have *revised The Tempest* after all his other plays were written, and inserted the passage where Prospero abjures his "rough magic," and buries his staff, and drowns his book. But I can hardly think that Shakespeare had any reference to himself in that passage: for, besides that he did not use to put his own feelings and purposes into the mouth of his characters, the doing so in this case would infer such a degree of self-exultation as, it seems to me, his native and habitual modesty would scarce permit.

Shakespeare was so unconscious of his great inventive faculty, so unambitious of originality in his plots and materials, and so apt to found his plays upon some popular chronicle or tale or romance, that he is generally, perhaps justly, presumed to have done so in this instance. Yet no play or novel has been identified as having furnished, in any sort, the basis of *The Tempest*, or any materials towards the composition. Commentators have been very diligent and inquisitive in the search; still, for aught appears thus far, the probability is, that, in this case, the plot had its origin in the Poet's mind. Collins the poet, indeed, told Thomas Warton that he had met with a novel called *Aurelio and Isabella*, dated 1588, and printed in Italian, Spanish, French, and English, upon which he thought *The Tempest* to have been founded: but poor Collins was at the time suffering under his mental disorder; and, as regards the particular novel he mentioned, his memory must have been at fault; for the story of Aurelio and Isabella has nothing in common with the play.

In the year 1841, however, Mr. Thoms called attention, in *The New Monthly Magazine*, to some remarkable coincidences between *The Tempest* and a German dramatic piece entitled *The Beautiful Sidea*, composed by Jacob Ayrer, who was a notary of Nuremberg, and contemporary with Shakespeare. In this piece, Prince Ludolph and Prince Leudegast answer to Prospero and Alonso. Ludolph is a magician, has an only daughter, Sidea, and an attendant spirit, Runcifal, who has some points of resemblance to Ariel. Soon after the opening of the piece, Ludolph, having been vanquished by his rival, and driven with his daughter into a forest, rebukes her for complaining of their change of fortune; and then summons his spirit Runcifal, in order to learn from him their future destiny, and their prospects of revenge. Runcifal, who, like Ariel, is somewhat "moody," announces to Ludolph that the son of his enemy will shortly become his prisoner. After a comic episode, Prince Leudegast, with his son Engelbrecht and the counsellors, is seen hunting in the same forest, when Engelbrecht and his companion Famulus, having separated from their associates, are suddenly encountered by Ludolph and his daughter. He commands them to yield themselves prisoners; they refuse, and attempt to draw their swords, when he renders them powerless by a touch of his magical wand, and gives Engelbrecht over to Sidea, to carry logs of wood for her, and to obey her in all things. Later in the piece, Sidea, moved with pity for the prince's labour in carrying logs, declares that she would "feel great joy, if he would prove faithful to me, and take me in wedlock"; an event which is at last happily brought to pass, and leads to a reconciliation of their parents.

Here the resemblances are evidently much too close to have been accidental: either the German must have borrowed from Shakespeare, or Shakespeare from the German, or both of them from some common source. Tieck gave it as his opinion that the German was derived from an English original now lost, to which Shakespeare was also indebted for the incidents of *The Tempest.* There the matter has to rest for the present.—There is, besides, an old ballad called *The Inchanted Island,* which was once thought to have contributed something towards the play: but it is now generally held to be more modern than the play, and probably founded upon it; the names and some of the incidents being varied, as if on purpose to disguise its connection with a work that was popular on the stage.

There has been considerable discussion as to the scene of *The Tempest.* A wide range of critics from Mr. Chalmers to Mrs. Jameson have taken for granted that the Poet fixed his scene in the Bermudas. For this they have alleged no authority but his mention of "the still-vex'd Bermoothes." Ariel's trip from "the deep nook to fetch dew from the still-vex'd Bermoothes" does indeed show that the Bermudas were in the Poet's mind; but then it also shows that his scene was not there; for it had been no feat at all worth mentioning for Ariel to fetch dew from one part of the Bermudas to another. An aerial voyage of some two or three thousand miles was the least that so nimble a messenger could be expected to make any account of. Besides, in less than an hour after the wrecking of the King's ship, the rest of the fleet are said to be upon the Mediterranean, "bound sadly home from Naples." On the other hand, the Rev. Mr. Hunter is very positive that, if we read the play with a map before us, we shall bring up at the island of Lampedusa, which "lies midway between Malta and the African coast." He makes out a pretty fair case, nevertheless I must be excused; not so much that I positively reject his theory as that I simply do not care whether it be true or not. But, if we must have any supposal about it, the most reasonable as well as the most poetical one seems to be, that the Poet, writing without a map, placed his scene upon an island of the mind; and that it suited his purpose to transfer to his ideal whereabout some of the wonders of Transatlantic discovery. I should almost as soon think of going to history for the characters of Ariel and Caliban, as to geography for the size, locality, or whatsoever else, of their dwelling-place. And it is to be noted that the old ballad just referred to seems to take for granted that the island was but an island of the mind; representing it to have disappeared upon Prospero's leaving it:

> From that day forth the isle has been
> By wandering sailors never seen:
>   Some say 'tis buried deep
> Beneath the sea, which breaks and roars
> Above its savage rocky shores,
>   Nor e'er is known to sleep.

HENRY HUDSON

1880.

Introduction

The Tempest, like most of Shakespeare's later plays, was first printed in the Folio edition of 1623, where it occupies the first place. It had then been, for at least ten years, one of his most popular and reputed pieces.

It was among the eighteen plays (six at least of them by Shakespeare) chosen for performance during the wedding festivities of the Palsgrave and the Princess Elizabeth in February 1613.[1] Beyond this fact we have no direct evidence of its date.[2] But it is extremely probable that the title contains an allusion to a tempest which wrecked Sir George Somers' ship, the 'Sea Venture,' in July 1609; and that various circumstances are drawn from the narratives afterwards published by Silvester Jourdain, one of the survivors, in October 1610, and by William Strachey, at a date which has not been precisely determined. The limits—October 1610 and February 1613—thus arrived at, are entirely confirmed by the internal evidence.

In style and metre *The Tempest* shares all the characteristics which place *Pericles*, *The Winter's Tale*, and *Cymbeline* very near the close of

---

[1] Lord Treasurer Stanhope's Accounts (quoted in *Century of Shakespeare's Praise*, p. 103). The exact number of Shakespeare's plays given depends upon the identification of 'Hotspur' with *Henry IV.* and of 'Sir John Falstaff' with this or *The Merry Wives*. He probably had a share also in the 'Cardenno.'

[2] In the Induction to his *Bartholomew Fair*, 1614, Ben Jonson delivered a passing gibe at 'those that beget Tales, *Tempests*, and such like Drolleries,' and 'If there be never a *Servant-master* i' the Fayre who can help it?' But this adds nothing to our knowledge.

Shakespeare's work. The same proneness to metrical movements which cross the normal verse-rhythm or enrich it with double endings;[3] the same abruptness of transition and elliptical brevity of phrase. Evident affinities of treatment, though less decisive, help to cement this connection: the separation and reunion of kin, the deliberate unreality of time and place, the bold implication of sea and storm in the web of the dramatic plot, the episodes of gracious idyll, the lofty humanity of the close. The one fragment of Shakespearean work clearly later in metrical character than *The Tempest* is his portion of *Henry VIII. The Winter's Tale* and *Cymbeline* cannot be later than 1611, when they were performed at the Globe most probably as new plays. *Henry VIII.* is known to have been a new play in 1613. *The Tempest* is therefore unlikely to have been produced much before or much after the earlier date.

This is the chief ground of hesitation in regard to the only really plausible counter-suggestion which has ever been made.[4] Dr. Garnett, taking up an idea already mooted by the older critics, but never before so effectively pushed home, holds that the recorded performance of *The Tempest* at the wedding festivities of the Princess Elizabeth was in reality the original one, that it was written expressly for the occasion, and that the circumstances of the marriage are allegorically figured in its plot. 'The foreign prince come from beyond sea, the island princess who has never left her home, the wise father who brings about the auspicious consummation of his policy; all found their counterparts among the splendid company that watched the performance on that February night.'[5] The parallel so far is striking, but it cannot be pursued much further without the aid of a somewhat questionable ingenuity. When, for example, a delicate allusion to the recent death of Prince Henry, the brother of the bride, is discovered in the supposed death of Ferdinand, the bridegroom—'the woe being by a consummate stroke of genius taken from Prospero the representative of James, and transferred to the house of his enemy,'—we suspect the hand of the critical necromancer who can make anything of anything. It may well be asked, too, whether a plot 'which revolves about the forcible expulsion of a ruler from his dominions and his daughter's wooing by the son of the usurper's chief ally,' was 'one that a shrewd dramatist would have chosen as the setting of an official epithalamium in honour of the

[3] The 'metrical tests' give *The Tempest* 35 per cent of double endings, 41 per cent of *enjambements*, 4.59 per cent of light or weak endings; the first is the highest proportion of all the plays, the second and third the highest but three.

[4] It is impossible to qualify this assertion in favour of the theory of Elze, who placed *The Tempest* in 1604, because Jonson in the prologue to *Volpone* (1605) referred to thefts from Montaigne (as if in allusion to Gonzalo's 'republic' in ii. 1). The earlier theory of Hunter, who identified *The Tempest* with the 'Love's Labour's Won' mentioned by Meres in 1598, is now quite out of count.

[5] *Universal Review*, April 1889.

daughter of a monarch so sensitive about his title to the crown as James I.'[6] And was the fanatical denouncer of 'those detestable slaves of the devil,—witches and enchanters'[7]—likely to appreciate the compliment of being 'represented' even by the most sublime magician in all literature?

It is, nevertheless, highly probable that The *Tempest* was designed to celebrate a marriage. A wedding masque occupies, with its insubstantial pageantry, the place of a strict dramatic crisis; and the hints of tragic harms, instead of being carried almost to the point of tragedy, as in The *Winter's Tale* and *Cymbeline*, are, like Ferdinand's log-piling, little more than a transparent make-believe. The real tragedy of Prospero's expulsion is an event already in the remote past when the action begins, and, though its results remain, they are so carefully denuded of pathetic suggestion that the island appears a very 'paradise of exiles.'

Nothing is known of the immediate source from which Shakespeare drew the story of *The Tempest*; but there is no doubt that it had already in substance been told. Among the waifs of historic tradition which drifted westward from the east of Europe was the story of Witold, a prince of Lithuania in the last quarter of the fourteenth century. Witold had resigned his government to a cousin Jagiello, who thereupon threw him into prison and handed over his capital, Wilna, to one Skirgiello. In 1388, however, Witold escaped with his daughter Sophia to Prussia, whence he carried on an indecisive struggle with Jagiello and Skirgiello for his inheritance. In this struggle he was supported by the avant-guard of eastern Christendom, the Teutonic Order; and in particular by the contingent of English soldiers who followed Henry Bolingbroke on one of those *Reisen* into Prussia, which were already familiar enough in England to be known by their German name.[8] Henry was thus brought into direct contact with Witold, and the Lithuanian prince found a place in the English chronicles which related the adventures of the future English king.[9]

Perhaps aided by this association with the Teutonic Order, the figure of the disinherited Lithuanian prince seems to have appealed to the romantic imagination of the West, and gathered a rich accretion of legendary traits. When we meet with him again two centuries later as

---

[6] S. Lee, *Diet, of Nat. Biog.* art. 'Shakespeare,' p. 379.

[7] James I.'s *Demonology*, Preface.

[8] Chaucer's knight 'reised in Lettowe.' The formation of the verb implies an extraordinary vogue; cf. the modern French and German *boycotter*, *boycotten*.

[9] Walsingham, *Hist. Anglicana.* Rolls ed. ii. 197-8. Witold appears as *Wytot*, Skirgiello as *Skirgall.* Knighton and Capgrave have briefer notices. All are quoted at length in Miss L. T. Smith's admirably edited accounts of *The Earl of Derby's Expeditions* (Camden Society, 1894). The connection with *The Tempest* was first made probable by Caro, *Englische Studien*, 1878.

the Prince Ludolff of Jacob Ayrer's drama *Die schöne Sidea*, he has become a magician, with an attendant spirit, Runcifal. Driven from his throne by his rival, Prince Leudegast, he takes refuge in the forest with his only daughter, Sidea. There one day he suddenly encounters Engelbrecht, the son of Leudegast, summons him to yield, and, on his resisting, charms his sword, paralyses his nerves, and compels him to carry logs for his daughter. Finally, after many irrelevant adventures, Engelbrecht marries Sidea, and their union brings about the reconciliation of the rival princes.

English actors were well acquainted with Nurnberg long before the date of *The Tempest*,[10] and Shakespeare may conceivably have heard some report of Ayrer's suggestive plot, though he assuredly had no opportunity of being repelled by its barbarous literary garb. But it is plain that, whether as floating tradition, or contemporary information, or in the form of some lost Elizabethan play, a story embodying all the points in which Ayrer anticipates *The Tempest*, served as material for the wonderful 'sea-change' there wrought.

The phrase is not without meaning, for half the fascination of the drama springs from the wild waters, roaring or allayed, which 'round' the enchanter's abode. Whatever rudiments of Prospero he may have found in tradition, Shakespeare first made his refuge an island, and the instrument of his revenge a storm. The story of the sea which caught the ear of England in 1610 perhaps supplied the first suggestion of the drama. Certainly it offered tempting coigns of vantage on which to lodge a story of enchantment. Many of its incidents, as told by Strachey and Jourdain, have evidently contributed to the description of the wreck and of the island. The admiral's ship, like Alonso's, was separated from his fleet and cast away, as the world for months believed, on the desolate island of 'Bermudas'; a spot 'never inhabited by any Christian or heathen people,' but only by 'witches and devils';[11] thence 'ever esteemed and reputed a most prodigious and inchanted place,'[12] habitually known as 'the Ile of Divels';[13] and not less dreaded for the 'accustomed monstrous thunderstorms and tempests'[14] by which it was 'still-vexed.' When, in October 1610, the actual story was published, it was discovered that the crew of the 'Sea Venture,' after giving up all for lost, had been saved as by miracle, the ship being 'driven and jammed between two rocks, fast lodged and locked for further budging,' so that all got ashore, contriving even to land 'many a bottle of beer,' and hogshead of oil and wine. Actual marvels were not wanting. For the admiral, being upon the watch on the night of the

[10] They are known to have acted there in 1604 and 1606. Ayrer died in 1605.
[11] Howe's continuation of *Stowe's Annals*, quot. By Delius.
[12] Jourdain.
[13] Jourdain's title.
[14] Howe's continuation of *Stowe's Annals*, quot. By Delius.

wreck, 'had an apparition of a little round light, like a faint star, trembling and streaming along with a sparkling blaze, half the height upon the main-mast, and shooting sometimes from shroud to shroud, tempting to settle as it were upon any of the four shrouds.'[15] Nevertheless, when the ship's company set foot upon the dreaded island, they found 'the ayre temperate . . . and the country abundantly fruitfull.'[16] But the 'divels' which they did not find they bred; for 'divers discontents nourished amongst us had like to have been the parents of bloody issues and mischiefs.'[17]

Something like a first sketch was here given of Shakespeare's shipwreck, a hint of the bickerings and conspiracies of the crew, and some elementary suggestions of the island scenery. Here, for the first and last time, Shakespeare touched that world of sea-marvel which it was reserved for the poet of *The Ancient Mariner* finally to annex to English poetry. The sea-wonders of the inland-bred poet are not evolved, like those of Coleridge, from the horrors of solitary wandering in 'a wide, wide sea.' They belong to the sea only in its dealings with the shore, to the seafarer only in his dealings with strange lands. Elves and sea-nymphs dance with printless foot upon the yellow sands and toll the knell of the drowned; unseen spirits mock the stranded seamen with the semblance of baying watchdogs and crowing cocks in farms on shore. And all the subtle poetic suggestiveness of the enchanted legend of the Bermudas seems to have been cunningly distilled in Ariel—the spirit of wind and fire, who sweeps the ship irresistibly to its 'deep nook' on the shore, and 'flames amazement' on its masts.[18]

Shakespeare's island, however, is much more than a poetically sublimated 'Isle of Divels.'[19] To the supernatural prodigies of the uninhabited Bermudas was added a sample of the human wonders of the new world, of the aborigines and 'strange fishes' which the Elizabethan townsman gaped at as they were landed in the little havens of Dorset and Devon, or paid his ten doits to see in the booths of a country fair. Both aspects of the Isle are cunningly compounded and

---

[15] Strachey.

[16] Jourdain.

[17] Howe's continuation of *Stowe's Annals*, quot. by Delius.

[18] The name Ariel, glossed by Shakespeare as 'an ayrie spirit' may have been taken from the great popular repertory of supernatural lore, Heywood's *Hierarchy of Angels.* But the character is Shakespeare's own, 'Ariel' being there associated with 'Earth.'

[19] That it was not meant literally to be 'the Bermudas' or any other earthly island is obvious from the deliberate blending of the geography of the Mediterranean with the marvels of the Indies. Resolute efforts were made by the older critics to fix its site in Lampedusa (Hunter, Douce), Corcyra (Bell), or the Bermudas, from which last in i. 2. 229 it is expressly distinguished.

transcended in the 'fishlike man-monster, offspring of a devil and a witch.'[20]

Into this scenery Shakespeare has transported the traditional story of the banished prince, blending them in a marvellously harmonious whole. The haunted island is subdued to the art of Prospero, and an undisciplined democracy of irresponsible spirits turned into a despotically ordered realm. Ariel becomes his minister and Caliban his slave, and his enemies from first to last are merely automatons of his art. Power so absolute, so unshadowed by a suspicion of remorse or fear, belongs to romance rather than to drama. In this romantic absoluteness Prospero differs from all other enchanters of the Elizabethan stage. There is as little trace in him of the tragic compunctions and misdoubts of Faustus as of the impostures of Jonson's Alchemist. Nor does it occur to any one in the drama to question the lawfulness of his art. Antonio himself had never thought, like Caliban in Renan's brilliant sequel, of inviting the Inquisition to deal with the secret student of necromancy. But Prospero is detached as completely from the traditional aims of magic as from its actual perils. If he was originally prompted to it, like Faustus, by the Humanist's passion for knowledge and power, he has long been emancipated, as Faustus never is, from the egoism of either passion, and uses his giant's strength, like adivine providence, first to bring a crew of criminals to justice, and then to extend to them the 'rarer virtue of mercy.' Before this, in tragedy, and in the quasi-tragic comedy of *Measure for Measure*, Shakespeare had drawn with pathos, or with irony, the endeavours of a Brutus, or a Vincentio, to take arms against evil. Prospero, the creation of a serener mood, clearly stands on a different plane of reality. More daringly detached from experience than any other purely human character in Shakespeare, he is drawn with a seriousness of conviction, and charged with a wealth of ethical suggestion, which belong in poetry only to the σκίαι τῶν ὄντων, the shadows of things that are. That more is symbolised than expressed in him every one feels. It is rash to define too peremptorily Shakespeare's thoughts; but that wonderful first decade of the seventeenth century, which had witnessed Shakespeare's achieved creation and Bacon's hardly less stupendous vision of discovery, could hardly have found an apter emblematic close.

Prospero makes the enchantments of the island the instruments of his art; its new-world simplicity is a condition of Miranda's virginal charm. That it was not the sole or the chief condition is thrust upon us

[20] The name of Sycorax has not been explained. W. W. Lloyd too learnedly interpreted it as *ψυχορρήξ*, 'heart-breaker.' Lamb identified her with a historical witch of Algiers. The name Setebos was taken from Eden's *History of Travayle* (1577), where it is the name of a Patagonian god. Several of the names of the shipwrecked courtiers likewise occur there.

with almost violent emphasis in the contrasted picture of Caliban, bred in the same island and by the same hand, but void of the saving birthright of noble race and inherited civility, so that upon his nature 'Nurture will never stick.' This contrast has a kind of inverted counterpart in the several groups of the wrecked crew—samples of civilised breeding at its best and worst;—from Ferdinand, almost the peer of Miranda, and 'holy' Gonzalo, the kindly friend of Prospero, to the traitors, Antonio and Sebastian, and the dregs of humanity, Stephano and Trinculo, in whose vulgar cynicism Caliban himself, with his pathetic awe, his naive poetry of wonder, finds a foil.

The slightness of its plot-interest has not prevented *The Tempest* from exercising a fascination upon posterity which in kind and variety belongs to no other play. It combines the profound and inexhaustible intellectual suggestiveness of *Hamlet* with the enchanted scenery, the piquant invention, the lyrical loveliness of the *Midsummer-Night's Dream.* It amused Pepys by its 'innocence,' and furnished new instruments of expression to a Browning and a Renan.

In its own century *The Tempest* served to some extent as an early edition of *Robinson Crusoe.* The honours of fame were fairly divided between Miranda and Caliban. 'The woman who had never seen a man' was a piquant conception, over which Fletcher in *The Sea Voyage* and Sir John Suckling in *The Goblins* (pr. 1646) drew the trail of their grosser fancy. After the Restoration it was witnessed by thronged houses with half-unwilling delight faithfully reflected in the naive records, already mentioned, of Pepys (1667-8). Dryden, nearly at the same time, paid *The Tempest* the ambiguous compliment of an adaptation in *The Enchanted Island* (produced in 1667, published in 1670). Nothing can better illustrate Shakespeare's admirable economy in the use of the marvels at his command, than this bustling composition of an ingenious playwright intent solely upon stage-effect. The banished Duke of Milan is doubled with an heir to the duchy of Mantua, and 'the woman who has never seen a man' with 'a man who has never seen a woman,' carefully secluded in another part of the cave. Ariel has a mistress, and Caliban a sister, Sycorax, who marries Trinculo. There is much cleverness in all this, and some wisdom; for Dryden perfectly understood that, as he confessed in the Prologue,

> Shakespeare's magic could not copied be.

Twelve years later he showed by a masterly appreciation of Caliban (in *The Grounds of Criticism in Tragedy*, 1679) that he had penetrated further than any contemporary into the methods of that magic. In our own century no one has ventured, on this elaborate scale, to make good the economies of Shakespeare; but the unexhausted zest of single aspects of the Isle has repeatedly overpowered the usual reluctance of wise men to carry further the stories which Shakespeare left half told. The voyage home to Naples proved adventurous in the hands of F. C. Waldron, whose *The Virgin Queen*, a melodrama, appeared in 1797. But it is chiefly the story of Caliban that has arrested the imagination of modern Europe. The grovelling worshipper of drink and 'Freedom' became in the hands of Renan an embodiment of prosperous and unspiritual democracy; and Browning elicited from the poor cowerer before the terrors of his dam's god Setebos the subtlest expression of the being of 'natural theology.' And among the imaginative progeny of *The Tempest* must be reckoned a long line of critical interpretations, Darwin's discoveries threw a new light upon the manmonster, which Daniel Wilson exploited in his *Caliban, or The Missing Link* (1873). Politics, metaphysics, anthropology, literary history, have each been divined in the cloudy symbols of Shakespeare's high romance.[21] Few of these interpretations have had any vogue. One, however, the world by a common instinct refuses to resign: that which regards Shakespeare as having, in Prospero's epilogue, himself bidden farewell to the stage.

CHARLES HAROLD HERFORD

1903.

---

[21] Cf. the summary in Dowden's *Shakspere, His Mind and Art*, p. 424.

THE TEMPEST

Dramatis Personae

ALONSO, *King of Naples.*
SEBASTIAN, *his brother.*
PROSPERO, *the right Duke of Milan.*
ANTONIO, *his brother, the usurping Duke of Milan.*
FERDINAND, *son to the King of Naples.*
GONZALO, *an honest old counselor.*
ADRIAN, *Lord.*
FRANCISCO, *Lord.*
CALIBAN, *a savage and deformed slave.*
TRINCULO, *a jester.*
STEPHANO, *a drunken butler.*
MASTER OF A SHIP
BOATSWAIN
MARINERS
MIRANDA, *daughter to Prospero.*
ARIEL, *an airy spirit.*
Spirits appearing as IRIS, CERES, *and* JUNO
NYMPHS
REAPERS
Other Spirits attending on Prospero.

ACT I.

SCENE I.

On a Ship at sea. A Storm, with Thunder and Lightning.

[*Enter* MASTER *and* BOATSWAIN *severally.*]

MASTER. Boatswain!

BOATSWAIN. Here, master: what cheer?

MASTER. Good,[1] speak to the mariners: fall to't, yarely,[2] or we run ourselves aground: bestir, bestir. [*Exit.*]

[*Enter* MARINERS.]

BOATSWAIN. Heigh, my hearts! cheerly, cheerly, my hearts! yare, yare! Take in the topsail. Tend to the master's whistle. [*Exeunt* MARINERS.]—Blow, till thou burst thy wind,[3] if room enough![4]

[*Enter* ALONSO, SEBASTIAN, ANTONIO, FERDINAND, GONZALO, *and others.*]

ALONSO. Good boatswain, have care. Where's the master? Play the men.[5]

BOATSWAIN. I pray now, keep below.

ANTONIO. Where is the master, boatswain?

BOATSWAIN. Do you not hear him? You mar our labour: keep your cabins: you do assist the storm.

GONZALO. Nay, good, be patient.

BOATSWAIN. When the sea is. Hence! What cares these roarers for the name of king? To cabin: silence! trouble us not.

GONZALO. Good, yet remember whom thou hast aboard.

---

[1] Here, as in many other places, *good* is used just as we now use *well.* So a little after: "*Good,* yet remember whom thou hast aboard." Also in *Hamlet,* i. 1: "*Good* now, sit down, and tell me," &c.

[2] *Yarely* is *nimbly, briskly,* or *alertly.* So, in the next speech, *yare,* an imperative verb, is *be nimble,* or *be on the alert.* In North's Plutarch we have such phrases as "galleys not *yare* of steerage," and "ships light of *yarage*" and "galleys heavy of *yarage.*"

[3] In Shakespeare's time, the wind was often represented pictorially by the figure of a man with his cheeks puffed out to their utmost tension with the act of blowing. Probably the Poet had such a figure in his mind. So in *King Lear,* iii. 2: "Blow, winds, and *crack your cheeks*!"

[4] That is, "if *we have* sea-room enough." So in Pericles, iii. 1: "But *sea-room,* an the brine and cloudy billow kiss the Moon, I care not."

[5] Act with spirit, behave like men. So in 2 Samuel, x. 12: "Be of good courage, and let us *play the men* for our people."

BOATSWAIN. None that I more love than myself. You are a counsellor; if you can command these elements to silence, and work the peace of the present,[6] we will not hand a rope more; use your authority: if you cannot, give thanks you have lived so long, and make yourself ready in your cabin for the mischance of the hour, if it so hap.—Cheerly, good hearts!—Out of our way, I say. [*Exit.*]

GONZALO. I have great comfort from this fellow: methinks he hath no drowning mark upon him; his complexion[7] is perfect gallows. Stand fast, good Fate, to his hanging: make the rope of his destiny our cable, for our own doth little advantage. If he be not born to be hanged, our case is miserable. [*Exeunt.*]

[*Re-enter* BOATSWAIN.]

BOATSWAIN. Down with the top-mast![8] yare! lower, lower! Bring her to try with main-course.[9] [*A cry within.*] A plague upon this howling! they are louder than the weather or our office.[10]—

[*Re-enter* SEBASTIAN, ANTONIO, *and* GONZALO.]

Yet again! what do you here? Shall we give o'er and drown? Have you a mind to sink?

SEBASTIAN. A pox o' your throat, you bawling, blasphemous, incharitable dog!

BOATSWAIN. Work you then.

ANTONIO. Hang, cur! hang, you whoreson, insolent noisemaker! We are less afraid to be drown'd[11] than thou art.

GONZALO. I'll warrant him for drowning,[12] though the ship were no stronger than a nutshell and as leaky as an unstanched wench.[13]

---

[6] *Present* for *present time.* So in the Prayer-Book: "That those things may please Him which we do at this *present.*"

[7] *Complexion* was often used for *nature*, *native bent* or *aptitude.*

[8] Of this order Lord Mulgrave, a sailor critic, says, "The striking the top-mast was a new invention in Shakespeare's time, which he here very properly introduces. He has placed his ship in the situation in which it was indisputably right to strike the top-mast,—where he had not sea-room."

[9] This appears to have been a common nautical phrase. So in Hackluyt's *Voyages*, 1598: "And when the bark had way we cut the hauser, and so gat the sea to our friend, and *tried out* all the day *with our maine* course." Also in Smith's *Sea Grammar*, 1627: "Let us lie at *trie with our maine course.*" And Sir Walter Raleigh speaks of being "obliged to lye at trye with our maine course and mizen." *To lie at try* is to keep as close to the wind as possible.

[10] *Weather* for *storm.* "Their howling drowns both the roaring of the tempest and the commands of the officer," or "our official orders."

[11] "Less afraid *of being* drown'd." So the Poet often uses the infinitive gerundively, or like the Latin *gerund.*

BOATSWAIN. Lay her a-hold, a-hold! set her two courses![14] off to sea again; lay her off.

[*Re-enter* MARINERS, *wet.*]

MARINERS. All lost! to prayers, to prayers! all lost!

[*Exeunt.*]

BOATSWAIN. What, must our mouths be cold?
GONZALO. The king and prince at prayers! let's assist them, For our case is as theirs.
SEBASTIAN. I'm out of patience.
ANTONIO. We're merely[15] cheated of our lives by drunkards:
This wide-chapp'd rascal—would thou mightst lie drowning,
The washing of ten tides!
GONZALO. He'll be hang'd yet,
Though every drop of water swear against it
And gape at widest to glut him.[16]

[*A confused noise within.*]

Mercy on us!—We split, we split!—Farewell, my wife and children!—Farewell, brother!—We split, we split, we split! [*Exit* BOATSWAIN.]
ANTONIO. Let's all sink with the King.[17] [*Exit.*]

---

[12] *As to*, or *as regards*, drowning. A not uncommon use of *for.*—Gonzalo has in mind the old proverb, "He that is born to be hanged will never be drowned."

[13] The meaning of this may be gathered from a passage in Fletcher's *Mad Lover*: Chilias says to the Priestess, "Be quiet, and be *stanch* too; no *inundations*."

[14] A ship's *courses* are her largest lower sails; "so called," says Holt, "because they contribute most to give her way through the water, and thus enable her to feel the helm, and steer her *course* better than when they are not *set* or spread to the wind." Captain Glascock, another sailor critic, comments thus: "The ship's head is to be put leeward, and the vessel to be drawn off the land under that canvas nautically denominated the two courses." To *lay a ship a-hold* is to bring her to lie as near the wind as she can, in order to keep clear of the land, and get her out to sea. So Admiral Smith, in his *Sailors' Wordbook*: "A hold: A term of our early navigators, for bringing a ship close to the wind, so as to hold or keep to it."

[15] *Merely*, here, is *utterly* or *absolutely*. A frequent usage. So in *Hamlet*, i. 2: "Things rank and gross in nature possess it *merely*."

[16] *Glut* for *englut*; that is, *swallow up*.—*Widest* is here a monosyllable the same with many words that are commonly two syllables.

[17] This double elision of *with* and *the*, so as to draw the two into one syllable, is quite frequent, especially in the Poet's later plays. So before in this scene: "Bring her to try *wi' th'* main course." Single elisions for the same purpose, such as *by th'*, *for th'*, *to th'*, &c., are still more frequent. So in the first speech of the next scene: "Mounting *to th'* welkin's cheek."

SEBASTIAN. Let's take leave of him. [*Exit.*]

GONZALO. Now would I give a thousand furlongs of sea for an acre of barren ground, long heath, brown furze, any thing.[18] The wills above be done! but I would fain die a dry death.[19] [*Exit.*]

SCENE II.

The Island: before the Cell of PROSPERO.

[*Enter* PROSPERO *and* MIRANDA.]

MIRANDA. If by your art, my dearest father, you have
Put the wild waters in this roar, allay them.
The sky, it seems, would pour down stinking pitch,
But that the sea, mounting to the welkin's cheek,[20]
Dashes the fire out. O, I have suffered
With those that I saw suffer: a brave[21] vessel,
Who had, no doubt, some noble creature in her,
Dash'd all to pieces. O, the cry did knock
Against my very heart. Poor souls, they perish'd.
Had I been any god of power, I would
Have sunk the sea within the earth or e'er[22]
It should the good ship so have swallow'd and
The fraughting souls[23] within her.

PROSPERO. Be collected:

---

[18] *Ling, heath, broom,* and *furze* were names of plants growing on British barrens. So in Harrison's description of Britain, prefixed to Holinshed: "*Brome, heth, firze,* brakes, whinnes, *ling,* &c."

[19] The first scene of *The Tempest* is a very striking instance of the great accuracy of Shakespeare's knowledge in a professional science, the most difficult to attain without the help of experience. He must have acquired it by conversation with some of the most skilful seamen of that time. The succession of events is strictly observed in the natural progress of the distress described; the expedients adopted are the most proper that could have been devised for a chance of safety: and it is neither to the want of skill of the seamen or the bad qualities of the ship, but solely to the power of Prospero, that the shipwreck is to be attributed. The words of command are not only strictly proper, but are only such as point the object to be attained, and no superfluous ones of detail. Shakespeare's ship was too well manned to make it necessary to tell the seamen how they were to do it, as well as what they were to do.—LORD MULGRAVE.

[20] *Welkin* is *sky.* We have other like expressions; as," the cloudy cheeks of heaven," in *Richard the Second,* and "the wide cheeks o' the air," in *Coriolanus.*—The hyperbole of waves rolling sky-high occurs repeatedly.

[21] *Brave* is *fine* or *splendid*; like the Scottish braw. Repeatedly so in this play, as also elsewhere.

[22] *Or e'er* is *before* or *sooner than.* So in Ecclesiastes, xii. 6: "*Or ever* the silver cord be loosed."

[23] *Fraught* is an old form of *freight.* Present usage would require *fraughted.* In Shakespeare's time, the active and passive forms were very often used indiscriminately. So, here, "fraughting souls" is *freighted* souls, or souls on freight.

No more amazement:[24] tell your piteous heart
There's no harm done.
MIRANDA. O, woe the day!
PROSPERO. No harm.
I have done nothing but in care of thee,
Of thee, my dear one, thee, my daughter,—who
Art ignorant of what thou art, nought knowing
Of whence I am, nor that I am more better[25]
Than Prospero, master of a full poor cell,
And thy no greater father.
MIRANDA. More to know
Did never meddle[26] with my thoughts.
PROSPERO. 'Tis time
I should inform thee farther. Lend thy hand,
And pluck my magic garment from me.—So:

[*Lays down his robe.*]

Lie there, my art.[27]—Wipe thou thine eyes; have comfort.
The direful spectacle of the wreck, which touch'd
The very virtue of compassion in thee,
I have with such provision in mine art
So safely ordered that there is no soul[28]—
No, not so much perdition as an hair
Betid to any creature in the vessel
Which thou heard'st cry, which thou saw'st sink. Sit down;
For thou must now know farther.
MIRANDA. You have often
Begun to tell me what I am, but stopp'd
And left me to a bootless inquisition,
Concluding *Stay, not yet.*
PROSPERO. The hour's now come;
The very minute bids thee ope thine ear;
Obey and be attentive. Canst thou remember
A time before we came unto this cell?
I do not think thou canst, for then thou wast not

---

[24] The sense of *amazement* was much stronger than it is now. Here it is *anguish* or *distress* of mind.

[25] This doubling of comparatives occurs continually in all the writers of Shakespeare's time. The same with superlatives.

[26] To *meddle* is, properly, to *mix*, to *mingle*.

[27] Lord Burleigh, at night when he put off his gown, used to say, "Lie there, Lord Treasurer"; and, bidding adieu to all State affairs, disposed himself to his quiet rest.—FULLER'S *Holy State*.

[28] The sense is here left incomplete, and purposely, no doubt. Prospero has many like changes of construction in this part of the scene.

Out three years old.[29]
MIRANDA. Certainly, sir, I can.
PROSPERO. By what? by any other house or person?
Of any thing the image tell me that
Hath kept with thy remembrance.
MIRANDA. 'Tis far off
And rather like a dream than an assurance
That my remembrance warrants. Had I not
Four or five women once that tended me?
PROSPERO. Thou hadst, and more, Miranda. But how is it
That this lives in thy mind? What seest thou else
In the dark backward and abysm[30] of time?
If thou remember'st aught ere thou camest here,
How thou camest here thou mayest.[31]
MIRANDA. But that I do not.
PROSPERO. Twelve year since, Miranda, twelve year[32] since,
Thy father was the Duke of Milan and
A prince of power.
MIRANDA. Sir, are not you my father?
PROSPERO. Thy mother was a piece of virtue, and
She said thou wast my daughter; and thy father
Was Duke of Milan; and thou his only heir
And princess no worse issued.
MIRANDA. O the Heavens!
What foul play had we, that we came from thence?
Or blessed was't we did?
PROSPERO. Both, both, my girl:
By foul play, as thou say'st, were we heaved thence,
But blessedly holp[33] hither.
MIRANDA. O, my heart bleeds
To think o' the teen[34] that I have turn'd you to,
Which is from my remembrance! Please you, farther.
PROSPERO. My brother and thy uncle, call'd Antonio,—

---

[29] Not *fully* three years old. We have a like use of *out* in iv. 1: "But, play with sparrows, and be a boy right *out.*"

[30] *Abysm* is an old form of *abyss*; from the old French *abisme.*

[31] "If thou remember'st aught *ere* thou earnest here, thou mayst also remember *how* thou camest here."

[32] In words denoting time, space, and quantity, the singular form was often used with the plural sense. So we have *mile* and *pound* for *miles* and *pounds.*—In this line, the first *year* is two syllables, the second one. Often so with various other words, such as *hour*, *fire*, &c.

[33] *Holp* or *holpen* is the old preterite of *help*; occurring continually in *The Psalter*, which is an older translation of the Psalms than that in the Bible.

[34] *Teen* is an old word for *trouble*, *anxiety*, or *sorrow.* So in *Love's Labours Lost*, iv. 3: "Of sighs, of groans, of sorrow, and of *teen.*"

I pray thee, mark me,—that a brother should
Be so perfidious!—he whom next thyself
Of all the world I loved and to him put
The manage of my State;[35] as at that time
Through all the signories it was the first,[36]
And Prospero the prime duke, being so reputed
In dignity, and for the liberal arts
Without a parallel; those being all my study,
The government I cast upon my brother
And to my state grew stranger, being transported
And rapt in secret studies. Thy false uncle,—
Dost thou attend me?

MIRANDA. Sir, most heedfully.

PROSPERO.—Being once perfected how to grant suits,
How to deny them, who[37] t' advance and who
To trash for over-topping,[38] new created
The creatures that were mine, I say, or changed 'em,
Or else new form'd 'em; having both the key
Of officer and office,[39] set all hearts i' the state
To what tune pleased his ear; that[40] now he was
The ivy which had hid my princely trunk,
And suck'd my verdure out on't. Thou attend'st not.[41]

MIRANDA. O, good sir, I do.

PROSPERO. I pray thee, mark me.
I, thus neglecting worldly ends, all dedicated
To closeness and the bettering of my mind
With that which, but[42] by being so retired,
O'er-prized all popular rate,[43] in my false brother

---

[35] *Manage* for *management* or *administration.* Repeatedly so.

[36] *Signiory* for *lordship* or *principality.* Botero, in his *Relations of the World*, 1630, says, "Milan claims to be the first duchy in Europe."

[37] This use of *who* where present usage requires *whom* was not ungrammatical in Shakespeare's time.

[38] To *trash* for *overtopping* is to *check* the *overgrowth,* to reduce the exorbitancy. The word seems to have been a hunting-term for checking the speed of hounds when too forward; the *trash* being a strap or rope fastened to the dog's neck, and dragging on the ground. The sense of *clogging* or *keeping back* is the right antithesis to *advance.*

[39] "The *key* of officer and office" is the *tuning* key; as of a piano.

[40] *That* is here equivalent to *so that,* or *insomuch that.* Continually so in old poetry, and not seldom in old prose.

[41] The old gentleman thinks his daughter is not attending to his tale, because his own thoughts keep wandering from it; his mind being filled with other things,—the tempest he has got up, and the consequences of it. This absence or distraction of mind aptly registers itself in the irregular and broken style of his narrative.

[42] This is the exceptive *but,* as it is called, and has the force of *be out,* of which it is, indeed, an old contraction. So later in this scene: "And, *but* he's something stain'd with grief," &c.; where *but* evidently has the force of *except that.*

Awaked an evil nature; and my trust,
Like a good parent, did beget of him
A falsehood in its contrary as great
As my trust was; which had indeed no limit,
A confidence sans bound.[44] He being thus lorded,
Not only with what my revenue[45] yielded,
But what my power might else exact, like one
Who having into truth, by telling of it,[46]
Made such a sinner of his memory,
To credit[47] his own lie, he did believe
He was indeed the duke; out o' the substitution,[48]
And executing the outward face of royalty,
With all prerogative: hence his ambition growing,—
Dost thou hear?[49]

MIRANDA. Your tale, sir, would cure deafness.

PROSPERO. To have no screen between this part he play'd
And him he play'd it for,[50] he needs will be
Absolute Milan. Me,[51] poor man, my library
Was dukedom large enough: of temporal royalties
He thinks me now incapable; confederates—
So dry he was for sway[52]—wi' the King of Naples
To give him annual tribute, do him homage,

---

[43] The meaning seems to be, "Which would have exceeded all popular estimate, but that it withdrew me from my public duties"; as if he were sensible of his error in getting so "rapt in secret studies" as to leave the State a prey to violence and usurpation.

[44] *Sans* is the French equivalent for *without.* The Poet uses it whenever he wants a monosyllable with that meaning.

[45] Shakespeare, in a few instances, has *revenue* with the accent on the first syllable, as in the vulgar pronunciation of our time. Here the accent is on the second syllable, as it should be.

[46] The verb to *false* was often used for to *treat falsely*, to *falsify*, to *forge*, to *lie.* So in *Cymbeline*, ii. 3: "And make Diana's rangers *false* themselves." And in *The Faerie Queene*, ii. 1, 1: "Whom Princes late displeasure left in bands, for *falsed* letters." Also in i. 3, 30: "And in his *falsed* fancy he her takes to be the fairest wight," &c. And in Drant's Horace: "The taverner that *falseth* othes, and little reckes to lye."—The pronoun *it* may refer to *truth*, or may be used absolutely; probably the former. The Poet has such phrases as to *prince it*, for to *act the prince*, and to *monster it*, for to *be a monster.* And so the word is often used now in all sorts of speech and writing; as to *braze it out*, and to *foot it through.*

[47] "*As* to credit" is the meaning. The Poet often omits *as* in such cases. Sometimes he omits both of the correlatives *so* and *as.*

[48] That is, "*in consequence* of his being my substitute or deputy."

[49] In this place, *hear* was probably meant as a dissyllable; just as *year* a little before. So, at all events, the verse requires.

[50] This is well explained by Mr. P. A. Daniel: "Prospero was the screen behind which the traitorous Antonio governed the people of Milan; and, to remove this screen between himself and them, he conspired his brother's overthrow."

[51] "*For* me" is the meaning. Such ellipses are frequent.

[52] So *thirsty* for power or rule; no uncommon use of *dry* now.

Subject his coronet to his crown and bend
The dukedom yet unbow'd—alas, poor Milan!—
To most ignoble stooping.
MIRANDA. O the heavens!
PROSPERO. Mark his condition and the event;[53] then tell me
If this might be a brother.
MIRANDA. I should sin
To think but nobly[54] of my grandmother:
Good wombs have borne bad sons.
PROSPERO. Now the condition.
The King of Naples, being an enemy
To me inveterate, hearkens my brother's suit;
Which was, that he, in lieu o' the premises,[55]—
Of homage and I know not how much tribute,
Should presently extirpate me and mine
Out of the dukedom and confer fair Milan
With all the honours on my brother: whereon,
A treacherous army levied, one midnight
Fated to th' practice,[56] did Antonio open
The gates of Milan, and, i' the dead of darkness,
The ministers for the purpose hurried thence
Me and thy crying self.
MIRANDA. Alack, for pity!
I, not remembering how I cried out then,
Will cry it o'er again: it is a hint[57]
That wrings mine eyes to't.
PROSPERO. Hear a little further
And then I'll bring thee to the present business
Which now's upon's; without the which this story
Were most impertinent.[58]
MIRANDA. Wherefore did they not
That hour destroy us?
PROSPERO. Well demanded, wench:[59]
My tale provokes that question. Dear, they durst not,—

---

[53] *Condition* is the terms of his compact with the King of Naples; *event*, the consequences that followed.

[54] "*But* nobly" is *otherwise than* nobly. *To think* for *in thinking*. Another instance of the gerundial infinitive. See page 19, note 11.

[55] *In lieu of* is *in return for*, or *in consideration of*. Shakespeare never uses the phrase in its present meaning, *instead of*.

[56] *Plot, stratagem, contrivance* are old meanings of *practice*.

[57] *Hint* for *cause* or *theme*. A frequent usage. So again in ii. 1: "Our *hint* of woe is common."

[58] *Impertinently irrelevant*, or *out of place*; *not pertinent*; the old meaning of the word. The Poet never uses *irrelevant*.

[59] *Wench* was a common term of affectionate familiarity.

So dear the love my people bore me—set
A mark so bloody on the business, but
With colours fairer painted their foul ends.
In few,[60] they hurried us aboard a bark,
Bore us some leagues to sea; where they prepared
A rotten carcass of a boat, not rigg'd,
Nor tackle, sail, nor mast; the very rats
Instinctively had quit it: there they hoist us,[61]
To cry to the sea that roar'd to us, to sigh
To the winds whose pity, sighing back again,
Did us but loving wrong.

MIRANDA. Alack, what trouble
Was I then to you!

PROSPERO. O, a cherubim
Thou wast that did preserve me. Thou didst smile.
Infused with a fortitude from heaven,
When I have degg'd[62] the sea with drops full salt,
Under my burthen groan'd; which raised in me
An undergoing stomach,[63] to bear up
Against what should ensue.

MIRANDA. How came we ashore?

PROSPERO. By Providence divine.
Some food we had and some fresh water that
A noble Neapolitan, Gonzalo,
Out of his charity, being then appointed
Master of this design, did give us, with
Rich garments, linens, stuffs and necessaries,
Which since have steaded much;[64] so, of his gentleness,
Knowing I loved my books, he furnish'd me
From mine own library with volumes that
I prize above my dukedom.

MIRANDA. Would I might
But ever see that man!

---

[60] That is, in few *words*, in *short.* Often so.

[61] *Hoist* for *hoisted*; as, a little before, *quit* for *quitted.* So in *Hamlet*, iii. 4: "'Tis the sport to have the engineer *hoist* with his own petar." The Poet has many preterites so formed. And the same usage occurs in *The Psalter*; as in the 93d Psalm: "The floods are risen, O Lord, the floods have *lift* up their voice."

[62] To *deg* is an old provincial word for to *sprinkle.* So explained in Carr's *Glossary*: "To *deg* clothes is to sprinkle them with water previous to ironing." And in Atkinson's *Glossary of the Cleveland Dialect*, *degg* or *dagg* is explained "to sprinkle with water, to drizzle." Also, in Brockett's *Glossary of North-Country Words*: "*Dag*, a drizzling rain, dew upon the grass."—The foregoing quotations are from the Clarendon edition.

[63] An *undergoing stomach* is an *enduring courage.* Shakespeare uses *stomach* repeatedly for *courage.*

[64] Have stood us in good stead, or done us much service.

PROSPERO. Now I arise:[65]
Sit still, and hear the last of our sea-sorrow.
Here in this island we arrived; and here
Have I, thy schoolmaster, made thee more profit[66]
Than other princesses can that have more time
For vainer hours and tutors not so careful.
MIRANDA. Heavens thank you for't! And now, I pray you, sir,
For still 'tis beating in my mind, your reason
For raising this sea-storm?
PROSPERO. Know thus far forth.
By accident most strange, bountiful Fortune,
Now my dear lady, hath mine enemies
Brought to this shore; and by my prescience
I find my zenith[67] doth depend upon
A most auspicious star, whose influence
If now I court not but omit, my fortunes
Will ever after droop. Here cease more questions:
Thou art inclined to sleep; 'tis a good dulness,
And give it way: I know thou canst not choose.—

[MIRANDA *sleeps*.]

Come away, servant, come. I am ready now.
Approach, my Ariel, come.

[*Enter* ARIEL.]

ARIEL. All hail, great master! grave sir, hail! I come
To answer thy best pleasure; be't to fly,
To swim, to dive into the fire, to ride
On the curl'd clouds, to thy strong bidding task
Ariel and all his quality.[68]

---

[65] These words have been a great puzzle to the editors, and various explanations of them have been given. Staunton prints them as addressed to Ariel, and thinks this removes the difficulty. So taken, the words are meant to give Ariel notice that the speaker is now ready for his services in charming Miranda to sleep. But this does not seem to me very likely, as it makes Prospero give Ariel a second notice, in his next speech. So I rather adopt the explanation of Mr. Aldis Wright, who thinks Prospero means that "the crisis in his own fortunes has come"; that he is now about to emerge from the troubles of which he has been speaking; and that he regards this "reappearance from obscurity as a kind of resurrection, like the rising of the Sun." This view is fully approved by Mr. Joseph Crosby.

[66] *Profit* is here a verb: "Have *caused* thee to profit more," &c.

[67] The common explanation of this is, "In astrological language *zenith* is the *highest point* in one's fortunes." But I much prefer Mr. Crosby's explanation, who writes me as follows: "Note, here, the blending of ideas by the speaker: he means to say, 'My fortune depends upon a star which, being now in its zenith, is auspicious to me.'"

PROSPERO. Hast thou, spirit,
    Perform'd to point[69] the tempest that I bade thee?
ARIEL. To every article.
    I boarded the king's ship; now on the beak,
    Now in the waist,[70] the deck, in every cabin,
    I flamed amazement: sometime I'd divide,
    And burn in many places; on the topmast,
    The yards and bowsprit, would I flame distinctly,[71]
    Then meet and join. Jove's lightnings, the precursors
    O' the dreadful thunder-claps, more momentary[72]
    And sight-outrunning were not; the fire and cracks
    Of sulphurous roaring the most mighty Neptune
    Seem to besiege and make his bold waves tremble,
    Yea, his dread trident shake.
PROSPERO. My brave spirit!
    Who was so firm, so constant, that this coil[73]
    Would not infect his reason?
ARIEL. Not a soul
    But felt a fever of the mad,[74] and play'd
    Some tricks of desperation. All but mariners
    Plunged in the foaming brine and quit the vessel,
    Then all afire with me: the king's son, Ferdinand,
    With hair up-staring,[75]—then like reeds, not hair,—
    Was the first man that leap'd; cried, *Hell is empty*
    And all the devils are here.
PROSPERO. Why that's my spirit!
    But was not this nigh shore?
ARIEL. Close by, my master.
PROSPERO. But are they, Ariel, safe?
ARIEL. Not a hair perish'd;
    On their unsustaining[76] garments not a blemish,

---

[68] That is, all of his *kind*, all his *fellow-spirits*, or who are like him.

[69] Perform'd *exactly*, or in *every point*; from the French *a point.*

[70] *Beak*, the prow of the ship; *waist*, the part between the quarter-deck and forecastle.

[71] So in the account of Robert Tomson's voyage, 1555, quoted by Mr. Hunter: "This light continued aboard our ship about three hours, flying from mast to mast, and from top to top; and sometimes it would be in two or three places at once." In the text, *distinctly* has the sense of *separately*; flaming in different places at the same time.

[72] *Momentary* in the sense of *instantaneous.*

[73] *Coil* is *stir, tumult*, or *disturbance.*

[74] Such a fever as madmen feel when the frantic fit is on them.

[75] *Upstaring* is *sticking out* "like quills upon the fretful porpentine." So in *The Faerie Queene*, vi. 11, 27: "With ragged weedes, and *locks upstaring* hye." And in *Julius Cæsar*, iv. 3: "Art thou some god, some angel, or some devil, that makest my blood cold, and my hair to *stare*?"

But fresher than before: and, as thou badest me,
In troops I have dispersed them 'bout the isle.
The king's son have I landed by himself;
Whom I left cooling of the air with sighs
In an odd angle of the isle,[77] and sitting,
His arms in this sad knot.[78]

PROSPERO. Of the king's ship
The mariners say how thou hast disposed
And all the rest o' the fleet.

ARIEL. Safely in harbour
Is the king's ship; in the deep nook, where once
Thou call'dst me up at midnight to fetch dew
From the still-vex'd Bermoothes,[79] there she's hid:
The mariners all under hatches stow'd;
Who, with a charm join'd to their suffer'd labour,
I have left asleep; and for the rest o' the fleet
Which I dispersed, they all have met again
And are upon the Mediterranean flote,[80]
Bound sadly home for Naples,
Supposing that they saw the king's ship wreck'd
And his great person perish.

PROSPERO. Ariel, thy charge
Exactly is perform'd: but there's more work.
What is the time o' the day?

ARIEL. Past the mid season.
At least two glasses.[81]

PROSPERO. The time 'twixt six and now
Must by us both be spent most preciously.

ARIEL. Is there more toil? Since thou dost give me pains,

---

[76] *Unstaining* for *unstained*; another instance of the indiscriminate use of active and passive forms. This usage, both in participles and adjectives, is frequent all through these plays. So, in *The Winter's Tale*, iv. 4, we have "*discontenting* father "for *discontented* father; and in *Antony and Cleopatra*, iii. 13, "all-*obeying* breath" for *all-obeyed* breath, that is, breath that *all obey*. See, also, page 21, note 23.

[77] *Odd angle* is *insignificant* or *out-of-the way corner*.

[78] His arms folded up as in sorrowful meditation.

[79] *Still-vex'd* is *ever-troubled*. The Poet very often uses *still* in the sense of *ever* or *continually*. The Bermudas were supposed to be inhabited or haunted by witches and devils, and the sea around them to be agitated with perpetual storms. *Bermooth.es* was then the common spelling of *Bermudas*. So in Fletcher's *Women Pleased*, i. 2: "The Devil should think of purchasing that egg-shell, to victual such a witch for the Burmoothes." Also in Webster's *Duchess of Malfi*, iii. 2: "I would sooner swim to the Bermootha's on two politicians' rotten bladders."

[80] *Flote*, like the French *flot*, is *flood*, *wave*, or *sea*. This passage shows that the scene of the play is not laid in the Bermudas, as there has not been time for the rest of the fleet to sail so far. And Ariel's trip to fetch the dew mentioned above was a much greater feat than going from one part of the Bermoothes to another.

[81] *Two glasses* is *two runnings* of the hour-glass.

Let me remember[82] thee what thou hast promised,
Which is not yet perform'd me.
PROSPERO. How now? moody?
What is't thou canst demand?
ARIEL. My liberty.
PROSPERO. Before the time be out? no more!
ARIEL. I prithee,
Remember I have done thee worthy service;
Told thee no lies, made thee no mistakings, served
Without or grudge or grumblings: thou didst promise
To bate me a full year.
PROSPERO. Dost thou forget
From what a torment I did free thee?
ARIEL. No.
PROSPERO. Thou dost, and think'st it much to tread the ooze
Of the salt deep,
To run upon the sharp wind of the north,
To do me business in the veins o' the earth
When it is baked with frost.
ARIEL. I do not, sir.
PROSPERO. Thou liest, malignant thing![83] Hast thou forgot
The foul witch Sycorax, who with age and envy[84]
Was grown into a hoop? hast thou forgot her?
ARIEL. No, sir.
PROSPERO. Thou hast. Where was she born? speak; tell me.
ARIEL. Sir, in Argier.[85]
PROSPERO. O, was she so? I must
Once in a month recount what thou hast been,
Which thou forget'st. This damn'd witch Sycorax,
For mischiefs manifold and sorceries terrible
To enter human hearing, from Algiers,
Thou know'st, was banish'd: for one thing she had,[86]
They would not take her life. Is not this true?
ARIEL. Ay, sir.
PROSPERO. This blue-eyed hag[87] was hither brought with child

---

[82] *Remember* for *remind*, or *put in mind.* Often so.

[83] Prospero should not be supposed to say this in earnest: he is merely playing with his delicate and amiable minister.

[84] Here, as commonly in Shakespeare, *envy* is *malice*. And so he has *envious* repeatedly for *malicious*. The usage was common.

[85] *Argier* is the old English name for *Algiers.*

[86] What this one thing was, appears in Prospero's next speech.

[87] *Blue-eyed* and *blue eyes* were used, not for what we so designate, but for *blueness about the eyes.* So, in *As You Like It*, iii. 2, we have "a *blue eye*, and a sunken," to denote a gaunt, haggard, and cadaverous look. And so, in the text, *blue-eyed* is used as signifying

And here was left by the sailors. Thou, my slave,
As thou report'st thyself, wast then her servant;
And, for[88] thou wast a spirit too delicate
To act her earthy and abhorr'd commands,
Refusing her grand hests,[89] she did confine thee,
By help of her more potent ministers
And in her most unmitigable rage,
Into a cloven pine;[90] within which rift
Imprison'd thou didst painfully remain
A dozen years; within which space she died
And left thee there; where thou didst vent thy groans
As fast as mill-wheels strike.[91] Then was this island—
Save for the son that she did litter here,
A freckled whelp hag-born—not honour'd with
A human shape.
ARIEL. Yes, Caliban her son.
PROSPERO. Dull thing, I say so; he, that Caliban
Whom now I keep in service. Thou best know'st
What torment I did find thee in; thy groans
Did make wolves howl and penetrate the breasts
Of ever angry bears: it was a torment
To lay upon the damn'd, which Sycorax
Could not again undo: it was mine art,
When I arrived and heard thee, that made gape
The pine and let thee out.
ARIEL. I thank thee, master.
PROSPERO. If thou more murmur'st, I will rend an oak
And peg thee in his knotty entrails till
Thou hast howl'd away twelve winters.
ARIEL. Pardon, master;
I will be correspondent to command
And do my spiriting gently.
PROSPERO. Do so, and after two days
I will discharge thee.
ARIEL. That's my noble master!
What shall I do? say what; what shall I do?
PROSPERO. Go make thyself like a nymph o' the sea: be subject
To no sight but thine and mine, invisible

---

extreme ugliness. In the Poet's time, what we call *blue* eyes were commonly called *gray*, and were considered eminently beautiful.

[88] Here, as often, *for* is *because*.

[89] *Hests* is *commands*, *orders*, or *behests*.

[90] *Into* and *in* were often used indiscriminately. Here, however, I suspect the sense of both words is implied: "She thrust you *into* a *splitted* pine, and there fastened you *in*."

[91] The reference is to *wind-mills*, which made a great clatter.

To every eyeball else. Go take this shape
And hither come in't: go, hence with diligence!—[*Exit* ARIEL.]
Awake, dear heart, awake! thou hast slept well; Awake!
MIRANDA. [*Waking.*] The strangeness of your story put
Heaviness in me.
PROSPERO. Shake it off. Come on;
We'll visit Caliban my slave, who never
Yields us kind answer.
MIRANDA. 'Tis a villain, sir,
I do not love to look on.
PROSPERO. But, as 'tis,
We cannot miss him:[92] he does make our fire,
Fetch in our wood and serves in offices
That profit us. What, ho! slave! Caliban!
Thou earth, thou! speak.
CALIBAN. [*Within.*] There's wood enough within.
PROSPERO. Come forth, I say! there's other business for thee:
Come, thou tortoise! when![93]—

[*Re-enter* ARIEL, *like a Water-nymph.*]

Fine apparition! My quaint[94] Ariel,
Hark in thine ear.
ARIEL. My lord it shall be done. [*Exit.*]
PROSPERO. Thou poisonous slave, got by the devil himself
Upon thy wicked dam, come forth!

[*Enter* CALIBAN.]

CALIBAN. As wicked dew[95] as e'er my mother brush'd
With raven's feather from unwholesome fen
Drop on you both! a south-west blow on ye
And blister you all o'er![96]
PROSPERO. For this, be sure, to-night thou shalt have cramps,
Side-stitches that shall pen thy breath up; urchins[97]

---

[92] Cannot *do without* him, or cannot *spare* him. So in Lyly's *Euphues*: "Honey and wax, both so necessary that we cannot *miss* them."

[93] *When*! was in common use as an exclamation of impatience.

[94] *Ingenious*, *artful*, *adroit*, are old meanings of *quaint.*

[95] "*Wicked* dew" is, probably, dew that has been *cursed*, and so made *poisonous* or *baleful.*

[96] The Poet repeatedly ascribes a blighting virulence to the south-west wind; perhaps because, in England, that wind often comes charged with the breath of the Gulf-Stream. So he has "the south-fog rot him!" and "all the contagion of the south light on you!"

Shall, for that vast[98] of night that they may work,
All exercise on thee; thou shalt be pinch'd
As thick as honeycomb, each pinch more stinging
Than bees that made 'em.[99]

CALIBAN. I must eat my dinner.
This island's mine, by Sycorax my mother,
Which thou takest from me. When thou camest first,
Thou strok'st me and madest much of me, wouldst give me
Water with berries in't,[100] and teach me how
To name the bigger light, and how the less,
That burn by day and night: and then I loved thee
And show'd thee all the qualities o' the isle,
The fresh springs, brine-pits, barren place and fertile:
Cursed be I that did so! All the charms
Of Sycorax, toads, beetles, bats, light on you!
For I am all the subjects that you have,
Which first was mine own king: and here you sty me
In this hard rock, whiles you do keep from me
The rest o' the island.

PROSPERO. Thou most lying slave,
Whom stripes may move, not kindness! I have used thee,
Filth as thou art, with human care, and lodged thee
In mine own cell, till thou didst seek to violate
The honour of my child.

CALIBAN. O ho, O ho! would't had been done!
Thou didst prevent me; I had peopled else
This isle with Calibans.

PROSPERO. Abhorred slave,
Which any print of goodness wilt not take,
Being capable of all ill! I pitied thee,
Took pains to make thee speak, taught thee each hour

---

[97] *Urchins* were fairies of a particular class. Hedgehogs were also called *urchins*; and it is probable that the sprites were so named, because they were of a mischievous kind, the *urchin* being anciently deemed a very noxious animal.

[98] So in *Hamlet*, i. 2," in the dead *vast* and middle of the night"; meaning the silent void or vacancy of night, when spirits were anciently supposed to walk abroad on errands of love or sport or mischief.

[99] *Honeycomb* is here regarded as plural, probably in reference to the *cells* of which honeycomb is composed.

[100] It does not well appear what this was. Coffee was known, but, I think, not used, in England in Shakespeare's time. Burton, in his *Anatomy of Melancholy*, 1632, has the following: "The Turks have a drink called *coffa*, so named of a *berry* as black as soot, and as bitter." I suspect, however, that the Poet had juniper-berries in his mind. These, steeped in water, have a stimulating or exhilarating effect, which would no doubt be highly grateful to such a taste as Caliban manifests on drinking Stephano's wine. Hooker, in his *Vegetable Kingdom*, says, "The stimulating diuretic powers of the Savin, Juniperus Salina, are well known, and are partaken of in some degree by the common Juniper."

One thing or other: when thou didst not, savage,
Know thine own meaning,[101] but wouldst gabble like
A thing most brutish, I endow'd thy purposes
With words that made them known. But thy vile race,
Though thou didst learn, had that in't which good natures
Could not abide to be with; therefore wast thou
Deservedly confined into this rock,
Who hadst deserved more than a prison.
CALIBAN. You taught me language; and my profit on't
Is, I know how to curse. The red plague rid[102] you
For learning me your language!
PROSPERO. Hag-seed, hence!
Fetch us in fuel; and be quick, thou'rt best,
To answer other business. Shrug'st thou, malice?
If thou neglect'st or dost unwillingly
What I command, I'll rack thee with old[103] cramps,
Fill all thy bones with aches,[104] make thee roar
That beasts shall tremble at thy din.
CALIBAN. No, pray thee.—
[*Aside.*] I must obey: his art is of such power,
It would control my dam's god, Setebos,[105]
And make a vassal of him.
PROSPERO. So, slave; hence!

[*Exit* CALIBAN.]

[*Re-enter* ARIEL, *invisible, playing and singing*; FERDINAND *following.*]

---

[101] Did not attach any meaning to the sounds he uttered.

[102] *Rid* here means *destroy* or *dispatch.* So in *Richard the Second*, v. 4: "I am the King's friend, and will *rid* his foe."—Touching the "red plague," Halliwell quotes from *Practise of Physicke*, 1605: "Three different kinds of plague-sore are mentioned; sometimes it is *red*, otherwhiles yellow, and sometimes blacke, which is the very worst and most venimous."

[103] *Old* was much used simply as an intensive, just as *huge* often is now. The Poet has it repeatedly.

[104] *Ache* was formerly pronounced like the letter *H.* The plural, *aches*, was accordingly two syllables. We have many instances of such pronunciation in the old writers. So in *Antony and Cleopatra*, iv. 7: "I had a wound here that was like a T, but now 'tis made an H."

[105] *Setebos* was the name of an American god, or rather devil, worshipped by the Patagonians. In Eden's *History of Travaile*, 1577, is an account of Magellan's voyage to the South Pole, containing a description of this god and his worshippers; wherein the author says: "When they felt the shackles fast about their legs, they began to doubt; but the captain did put them in comfort and bade them stand still. In fine, when they saw how they were deceived, they roared like bulls, and cryed upon their *great devil Setebos*, to help them."

ARIEL's SONG.

Come unto these yellow sands,
And then take hands:
Courtsied when you have and kiss'd
The wild waves whist,[106]
Foot it featly here and there;
And, sweet sprites, the burthen bear.

Burden dispersedly.

Hark, hark! — Bow-wow!
The watch-dogs bark! — Bow-wow!
Hark, hark! I hear
The strain of strutting chanticleer — Cry, Cock-a-diddle-dow.

FERDINAND. Where should this music be? i' the air or the earth?
It sounds no more: and sure, it waits upon
Some god o' the island. Sitting on a bank,
Weeping again the king my father's wreck,
This music crept by me upon the waters,
Allaying both their fury and my passion[107]
With its sweet air: thence I have follow'd it,
Or it hath drawn me rather. But 'tis gone.
No, it begins again.
ARIEL. [*sings*.]

Full fathom five thy father lies;
Of his bones are coral made;
Those are pearls that were his eyes:
Nothing of him that doth fade
But doth suffer a sea-change[108]
Into something rich and strange.
Sea-nymphs hourly ring his knell:

BURDEN. Ding-dong.
Hark! now I hear them,—Ding-dong, bell.
FERDINAND. The ditty does remember my drown'd father.
This is no mortal business, nor no sound
That the Earth owes.[109] I hear it now above me.

---

[106] Soothed or charmed the raging waters into stillness or peace.

[107] *Passion* is here used in its proper Latin sense of *suffering*.

[108] Nothing fades *without undergoing* a sea-change. This use of *but* occurs repeatedly. So in *Hamlet*, i. 3: "Do not sleep *but let* me hear from you"; that is, "*without letting* me hear."

PROSPERO. The fringed curtains of thine eye advance,[110]
    And say what thou seest yond.
MIRANDA. What is't? a spirit?
    Lord, how it looks about! Believe me, sir,
    It carries a brave[111] form. But 'tis a spirit.
PROSPERO. No, wench; it eats and sleeps and hath such senses
    As we have, such. This gallant which thou seest
    Was in the wreck; and, but he's something stain'd
    With grief that's beauty's canker,[112] thou mightst call him
    A goodly person: he hath lost his fellows
    And strays about to find 'em.
MIRANDA. I might call him
    A thing divine, for nothing natural
    I ever saw so noble.
PROSPERO. [*Aside.*] It goes on, I see,
    As my soul prompts it.—Spirit, fine spirit! I'll free thee
    Within two days for this.
FERDINAND. Most sure, the goddess
    On whom these airs attend!—Vouchsafe my prayer
    May know if you remain upon this island;
    And that you will some good instruction give
    How I may bear me here: my prime request,
    Which I do last pronounce, is,—O you wonder!—
    If you be maid[113] or no?
MIRANDA. No wonder, sir;
    But certainly a maid.
FERDINAND. My language! Heavens!—
    I am the best of them that speak this speech,
    Were I but where 'tis spoken.
PROSPERO. How? the best?
    What wert thou, if the King of Naples heard thee?
FERDINAND. A single thing,[114] as I am now, that wonders

---

[109] *Owe* is *own, possess.* The old form of the word was *owen.* Abbott, in his *Shakespeare Grammar*, has the following: "In the general destruction of inflections which prevailed during the Elizabethan period, *en* was particularly discarded. So strong was the discarding tendency, that even the *n* in *owen*, to *possess*, was dropped, and Shakespeare continually uses *owe* for *owen*, or *own.* The *n* has now been restored."

[110] *Advance*, here, is *raise* or *lift up.* So in *Romeo and Juliet*, ii. 3: "Ere the Sun *advance* his burning eye." Especially used of lifting up military standards.

[111] *Brave*, again, for *fine* or *superb.* See page 21, note 21.

[112] Shakespeare uses *canker* in four different senses,—the *canker-worm*, the *dog-rose*, a malignant sore, *cancer*, and *rust* or *tarnish.* Here it probably means the last; as in St. James, v. 3: "Your gold and silver is *cankered*; and the *rust* of them shall be a witness against you."

[113] Ferdinand has already spoken of Miranda as a goddess: he now asks, if she be a mortal; not a celestial being, but a maiden. Of course her answer is to be taken in the same sense as his question. The name *Miranda* literally signifies *wonderful.*

To hear thee speak of Naples. He does hear me;
And that he does I weep: myself am Naples,
Who with mine eyes, never since at ebb, beheld
The king my father wreck'd.
MIRANDA. Alack, for mercy!
FERDINAND. Yes, faith, and all his lords; the Duke of Milan
And his brave son[115] being twain.
PROSPERO. [*Aside.*] The Duke of Milan
And his more braver daughter could control thee,[116]
If now 'twere fit to do't. At the first sight
They have changed eyes.—Delicate Ariel,
I'll set thee free for this.—A word, good sir;
I fear you have done yourself some wrong:[117] a word.
MIRANDA. Why speaks my father so ungently? This
Is the third man that e'er I saw, the first
That e'er I sigh'd for: pity move my father
To be inclined my way!
FERDINAND. O, if a virgin,
And your affection not gone forth, I'll make you
The Queen of Naples.
PROSPERO. Soft, sir! one word more.—
[*Aside.*] They are both in either's powers; but this swift business
I must uneasy make, lest too light winning
Make the prize light.—One word more; I charge thee
That thou attend me: thou dost here usurp
The name thou owest not; and hast put thyself
Upon this island as a spy, to win it
From me, the lord on't.
FERDINAND. No, as I am a man.
MIRANDA. There's nothing ill can dwell in such a temple:
If the ill spirit have so fair a house,
Good things will strive to dwell with't.
PROSPERO. [*To* FERDINAND.] Follow me.—
Speak not you for him; he's a traitor.—Come;
I'll manacle thy neck and feet together:
Sea-water shalt thou drink; thy food shall be

---

[114] The Poet repeatedly uses *single* for *weak* or *feeble*: here, along with this, it has the further sense of *solitary* or *companionless*. Ferdinand supposes himself to be the only one saved of all that were in the ship.

[115] This young man, the son of Antonio, nowhere appears in the play, nor is there any other mention of him.

[116] To *control* was formerly used in the sense of to *refute*; from the French *contre-roller*, to exhibit a *contrary account*. Prospero means that he could refute what Ferdinand has just said about the Duke of Milan.

[117] "Done wrong to your character, in claiming to be King of Naples." Or incurred the penalty of being a spy or an usurper, by assuming a title that does not belong to him.

The fresh-brook muscles, wither'd roots and husks
Wherein the acorn cradled. Follow.
FERDINAND. No;
I will resist such entertainment till
Mine enemy has more power.

[*Draws, and is charmed from moving.*]

MIRANDA. O dear father,
Make not too rash a trial of him, for
He's gentle and not fearful.[118]
PROSPERO. What? I say,
My foot my tutor?—Put thy sword up, traitor;
Who makest a show but darest not strike, thy conscience
Is so possess'd with guilt: come from thy ward;[119]
For I can here disarm thee with this stick
And make thy weapon drop.
MIRANDA. Beseech you, father!—
PROSPERO. Hence! hang not on my garments.
MIRANDA. Sir, have pity;
I'll be his surety.
PROSPERO. Silence! one word more
Shall make me chide thee, if not hate thee. What!
An advocate for an imposter! hush!
Thou think'st there is no more such shapes as he,
Having seen but him and Caliban: foolish wench!
To the most of men this is a Caliban
And they to him are angels.
MIRANDA. My affections
Are then most humble; I have no ambition
To see a goodlier man.
PROSPERO. [*To* FERDINAND.] Come on; obey:
Thy nerves[120] are in their infancy again
And have no vigour in them.
FERDINAND. So they are;
My spirits, as in a dream, are all bound up.
My father's loss, the weakness which I feel,

---

[118] This clearly means that Ferdinand is brave and high-spirited, so that, if pressed too hard, he will rather die than succumb. It is a good old notion that bravery and gentleness naturally go together.

[119] *Ward* is *posture* or *attitude of defence*. Ferdinand is standing with his sword drawn, and his body planted, ready for defending himself. So, in *1 Henry the Fourth*, ii. 4, Falstaff says, "Thou knowest my old *ward*: here I lay, and thus I bore my point."

[120] *Nerves* for *sinews*; the two words being used indifferently in the Poet's time. Also *artery*, as in *Hamlet*, i. 4: "And makes each petty *artery* as hardy as the Nemean lion's *nerve*."

The wreck of all my friends, nor this man's threats,
To whom I am subdued, are but light to me,
Might I but through my prison once a day
Behold this maid: all corners else o' the earth
Let liberty make use of; space enough
Have I in such a prison.

PROSPERO. [*Aside.*] It works.—[*To* FERDINAND.] Come on.—Thou hast done well, fine Ariel!—[*To* FERDINAND.] Follow me.—[*To* ARIEL.] Hark what thou else shalt do me.

MIRANDA. [*to* FERDINAND.] Be of comfort;
My father's of a better nature, sir,
Than he appears by speech: this is unwonted
Which now came from him.

PROSPERO. Thou shalt be free
As mountain winds: but then exactly do
All points of my command.

ARIEL. To th' syllable.

PROSPERO. Come, follow.—Speak not for him. [*Exeunt.*]

ACT II.

SCENE I.

Another Part of the Island.

[*Enter* ALONSO, SEBASTIAN, ANTONIO, GONZALO, ADRIAN, FRANCISCO, *and others.*]

GONZALO. Beseech you, sir, be merry; you have cause—
So have we all—of joy; for our escape
Is much beyond our loss. Our hint of woe
Is common; every day some sailor's wife,
The masters of some merchant,[121] and the merchant
Have just our theme of woe; but for the miracle—
I mean our preservation—few in millions
Can speak like us: then wisely, good sir, weigh
Our sorrow with our comfort.

ALONSO. Prithee, peace.

SEBASTIAN. He receives comfort like cold porridge.

ANTONIO. The visitor[122] will not give him o'er so.

---

[121] Meaning what we call a *merchant-vessel* or a *merchant-man.*

[122] He calls Gonzalo a *visitor* in allusion to the office of one who visits the sick or the afflicted, to give counsel and consolation. The caustic scoffing humour of Sebastian and Antonio, in this scene, is wisely conceived.

SEBASTIAN. Look he's winding up the watch of his wit; by and by it will strike.
GONZALO. Sir,—
SEBASTIAN. One:—tell.[123]
GONZALO.—When every grief is entertain'd that's offer'd,
Comes to the entertainer—
SEBASTIAN. A dollar.
GONZALO. Dolour comes to him, indeed: you have spoken truer than you purposed.
SEBASTIAN. You have taken it wiselier than I meant you should.
GONZALO. Therefore, my lord,—
ANTONIO. Fie, what a spendthrift is he of his tongue!
ALONSO. I prithee, spare.
GONZALO. Well, I have done: but yet,—
SEBASTIAN. He will be talking.
ANTONIO. Which, of he or Adrian,[124] for a good wager, first begins to crow?
SEBASTIAN. The old cock.
ANTONIO. The cockerel.
SEBASTIAN. Done. The wager?
ANTONIO. A laughter.
SEBASTIAN. A match!
ADRIAN. Though this island seem to be desert,—
ANTONIO. Ha, ha, ha!
SEBASTIAN. So, you're paid.[125]
ADRIAN.—uninhabitable and almost inaccessible,—
SEBASTIAN. Yet,—
ADRIAN.—yet—
ANTONIO. He could not miss't.
ADRIAN.—it must needs be of subtle, tender and delicate temperance.[126]
ANTONIO. Temperance was a delicate wench.
SEBASTIAN. Ay, and a subtle; as he most learnedly delivered.
ADRIAN. The air breathes upon us here most sweetly.
SEBASTIAN. As if it had lungs and rotten ones.

---

[123] *Tell* is *count*, or *keep tally*; referring to "the watch of his wit," which he was said to be "winding up," and which now begins to strike.

[124] This, it appears, is an old mode of speech, which is now entirely obsolete. Shakespeare has it once again. And Walker quotes an apposite passage from Sidney's *Arcadia*: "The question arising, who should be the first to fight against Phalantus, of the black or the ill-apparelled knight," &c.

[125] A laugh having been agreed upon as the wager, and Sebastian having lost, he now pays with a laugh.

[126] By *temperance* Adrian means *temperature*, and Antonio plays upon the word; alluding, perhaps, to the Puritan custom of bestowing the names of the cardinal virtues upon their children.

ANTONIO. Or as 'twere perfumed by a fen.

GONZALO. Here is everything advantageous to life.

ANTONIO. True; save means to live.

SEBASTIAN. Of that there's none, or little.

GONZALO. How lush[127] and lusty the grass looks! how green!

ANTONIO. The ground indeed is tawny.

SEBASTIAN. With an eye of green in't.[128]

ANTONIO. He misses not much.

SEBASTIAN. No; he doth but mistake the truth totally.

GONZALO. But the rarity of it is,—which is indeed almost beyond credit,—

SEBASTIAN. As many vouched rarities are.

GONZALO.—that our garments, being, as they were, drenched in the sea, hold notwithstanding their freshness and glosses, being rather new-dyed than stained with salt water.

ANTONIO. If but one of his pockets could speak, would it not say he lies?

SEBASTIAN. Ay, or very falsely pocket up his report.

GONZALO. Methinks our garments are now as fresh as when we put them on first in Afric, at the marriage of the king's fair daughter Claribel to the King of Tunis.

SEBASTIAN. 'Twas a sweet marriage, and we prosper well in our return.

ADRIAN. Tunis was never graced before with such a paragon to[129] their queen.

GONZALO. Not since widow Dido's time.

ANTONIO. Widow! a pox o' that! How came that *widow* in? widow Dido!

SEBASTIAN. What if he had said widower Æneas' too? Good Lord, how you take it!

ADRIAN. Widow Dido, said you? you make me study of that: she was of Carthage, not of Tunis.

GONZALO. This Tunis, sir, was Carthage.

ADRIAN. Carthage?

GONZALO. I assure you, Carthage.

ANTONIO. His word is more than the miraculous harp.[130]

---

[127] *Lush* is *juicy, succulent,*—luxuriant.

[128] A *tint* or *shade* of green. So in Sandy's *Travels*: "Cloth of silver, tissued with an *eye* of green;" and Bayle has "Red with an *eye* of blue."

[129] *To* was used in such cases where we should use *for* or *as*. So in the Marriage Office of the Church: "Wilt thou have this woman *to* thy wedded wife?" Also, in St. Mark, xii. 23: "The seven had her *to* wife."

[130] Amphion, King of Thebes, was a prodigious musician: god Mercury gave him a lyre, with which he charmed the stones into their places, and thus built the walls of the city: as Wordsworth puts it, "The gift to King Amphion, that wall'd a city with its melody." Tunis is in fact supposed to be on or near the site of ancient Carthage.

SEBASTIAN. He hath raised the wall and houses too.
ANTONIO. What impossible matter will he make easy next?
SEBASTIAN. I think he will carry this island home in his pocket and give it his son for an apple.
ANTONIO. And, sowing the kernels of it in the sea, bring forth more islands.
GONZALO. Ay.
ANTONIO. Why, in good time.
GONZALO. Sir, we were talking that our garments seem now as fresh as when we were at Tunis at the marriage of your daughter, who is now queen.
ANTONIO. And the rarest that e'er came there.
SEBASTIAN. Bate, I beseech you, widow Dido.
ANTONIO. O, widow Dido! ay, widow Dido.
GONZALO. Is not, sir, my doublet as fresh as the first day I wore it? I mean, in a sort.
ANTONIO. That sort was well fished for.[131]
GONZALO. When I wore it at your daughter's marriage?
ALONSO. You cram these words into mine ears against
The stomach of my sense.[132] Would I had never
Married my daughter there! for, coming thence,
My son is lost and, in my rate,[133] she too,
Who is so far from Italy removed
I ne'er again shall see her.—O thou mine heir
Of Naples and of Milan, what strange fish
Hath made his meal on thee?
FRANCISCO. Sir, he may live:
I saw him beat the surges under him,
And ride upon their backs; he trod the water,
Whose enmity he flung aside, and breasted
The surge most swoll'n that met him; his bold head
'Bove the contentious waves he kept, and oar'd
Himself with his good arms in lusty stroke
To the shore, that o'er his[134] wave-worn basis bow'd,
As[135] stooping to relieve him: I not doubt
He came alive to land.

---

[131] A punning allusion, probably, to one of the meanings of *sort*, which was *lot* or *portion*; from the Latin *sors*.

[132] That is, "when the state of my feelings does not relish them, or has no *appetite* for them." *Stomach* for *appetite* occurs repeatedly.

[133] *Rate* for *reckoning*, *account*, or estimation.

[134] *His* for *its*, referring to *shore*. In the Poet's time *its* was not an accepted word: it was then just creeping into use; and he has it occasionally, especially in his later plays; as it occurs once or twice in this play.

[135] Here *as* is put for *as if*, a very frequent usage with the Poet, as also with other writers of the time.

ALONSO. No, no, he's gone.
SEBASTIAN. Sir, you may thank yourself for this great loss,
That would not bless our Europe with your daughter,
But rather lose her to an African;
Where she at least is banish'd from your eye,
Who[136] hath cause to wet the grief on't.
ALONSO. Prithee, peace.
SEBASTIAN. You were kneel'd to and importuned otherwise
By all of us, and the fair soul herself
Weigh'd between loathness and obedience, at
Which end o' the beam should bow.[137] We have lost your son,
I fear, for ever: Milan and Naples have
More widows in them of this business' making
Than we bring men to comfort them:
The fault's your own.
ALONSO. So is the dear'st o' the loss.[138]
GONZALO. My lord Sebastian,
The truth you speak doth lack some gentleness
And time to speak it in: you rub the sore,
When you should bring the plaster.
SEBASTIAN. Very well.
ANTONIO. And most chirurgeonly.[139]
GONZALO. It is foul weather in us all, good sir,
When you are cloudy.[140]
SEBASTIAN. Foul weather?
ANTONIO. Very foul.
GONZALO. Had I plantation[141] of this isle, my Lord,—
ANTONIO. He'd sow't with nettle-seed.
SEBASTIAN. Or docks, or mallows.
GONZALO. And were the king on't, what would I do?
SEBASTIAN. 'Scape being drunk for want of wine.
GONZALO. I' the commonwealth I would by contraries

---

[136] *Who* and *which* were used indifferently both of persons and things. Here *who* refers to *eye.* And the meaning probably is, "your eye, which hath cause to sprinkle or water your grief with tears." This would of course make the grief grow stronger. "The grief *on't*" is the grief *arising from it* or *out of it*; that is, from the loss or banishment of Claribel.

[137] *Hesitated*, or *stood in doubt*, between *reluctance* and obedience, which way the balance should turn or incline. To *weigh* is to *deliberate*, and hence to pause, to be *in suspense*, or to suspend action.

[138] *Dear* was used of any thing that causes strong feeling, whether of pleasure or of pain; as it *hurts* us to lose that which is *dear* to us.

[139] *Chirurgeon* is the old word, which has got transformed into *surgeon.*

[140] The meaning is, "your *gloom* makes us all gloomy." A cloud in the face is a common metaphor both for anger and for sorrow.

[141] In Shakespeare's time a *plantation* meant a *colony*, and was so used of the American colonies. Here *plantation* is a "verbal noun," and means *the colonizing.*

Execute all things; for no kind of traffic
Would I admit; no name of magistrate;
Letters should not be known; riches, poverty,
And use of service, none; contract, succession,
Bourn, bound of land, tilth,[142] vineyard, none;
No use of metal, corn, or wine, or oil;
No occupation; all men idle, all;
And women too, but innocent and pure;
No sovereignty:—

SEBASTIAN. Yet he would be king on't.

ANTONIO. The latter end of his commonwealth forgets the beginning.

GONZALO. All things in common nature should produce
Without sweat or endeavour: treason, felony,
Sword, pike, knife, gun, or need of any engine,[143]
Would I not have; but nature should bring forth,
Of its own kind, all foison,[144]—all abundance,
To feed my innocent people.

SEBASTIAN. No marrying 'mong his subjects?

ANTONIO. None, man; all idle: whores and knaves.

GONZALO. I would with such perfection govern, sir,
To excel the golden age.[145]

SEBASTIAN. God save his majesty!

ANTONIO. Long live Gonzalo!

GONZALO. And,—do you mark me, sir?—

ALONSO. Prithee, no more: thou dost talk nothing to me.

GONZALO. I do well believe your highness; and did it to minister occasion to these gentlemen, who are of such sensible[146] and nimble lungs that they always use to laugh at nothing.

ANTONIO. 'Twas you we laughed at.

GONZALO. Who in this kind of merry fooling am nothing to you:[147] so you may continue and laugh at nothing still.

---

[142] *Succession* is the tenure of property by inheritance, as the son *succeeds* the father.—*Bourn* is *boundary* or *limit.* Properly it means a stream of water, river, rivulet, or brook; these being the most natural boundaries of landed property.—*Tilth* is *tillage*: also used of land tilled, or prepared for sowing. So in *Measure for* Measure, iv. 1: "Our corn's to reap, for yet our *tilth's* to *sow.*"

[143] *Engine* was applied to any kind of *machine*: here it probably means *furniture of war.*

[144] *Foison* is an old word for *plenty* or *abundance* of provision, especially of the fruits of the soil. Often used so by the Poet.

[145] "The golden age" is that fabulous period in "the dark backward of time" when men knew nothing of sin and sorrow, and were so wise and good as to have no need of laws and government. Milton, in his *Ode on the Nativity,* has "Time will run back, and fetch the *age of gold.*"

[146] *Sensible* for *sensitive.* So in *Coriolanus,* i. 3: "I would your cambric were *sensible* as your finger, that you might leave pricking it for pity."

[147] Nothing *in comparison with* you. So the Poet often uses *to.*

ANTONIO. What a blow was there given!
SEBASTIAN. An it had not fallen flat-long.[148]
GONZALO. You are gentlemen of brave mettle;[149] you would lift the moon out of her sphere, if she would[150] continue in it five weeks without changing.

[*Enter* ARIEL, *invisible, playing solemn music.*]

SEBASTIAN. We would so, and then go a bat-fowling.[151]
ANTONIO. Nay, good my lord, be not angry.
GONZALO. No, I warrant you; I will not adventure my discretion[152] so weakly. Will you laugh me asleep, for I am very heavy?
ANTONIO. Go sleep, and hear us.

[*All sleep except* ALONSO, SEBASTIAN, *and* ANTONIO.]

ALONSO. What, all so soon asleep! I wish mine eyes
Would, with themselves, shut up my thoughts: I find
They are inclined to do so.
SEBASTIAN. Please you, sir,
Do not omit the heavy offer of it:[153]
It seldom visits sorrow; when it doth,
It is a comforter.
ANTONIO. We two, my lord,
Will guard your person while you take your rest,
And watch your safety.
ALONSO. Thank you.—Wondrous heavy.

[ALONSO *sleeps. Exit* ARIEL.]

SEBASTIAN. What a strange drowsiness possesses them!
ANTONIO. It is the quality o' the climate.

---

[148] The idea is of a sword handled so awkwardly as to hit with the side, and not with the edge.

[149] *Brave mettle* is *high, glorious*, or *magnificent spirit.* The Poet often has *mettle* in that sense.—*Sphere*, in the next line, is *orbit.*

[150] Our present usage requires *should.* In Shakespeare's time, the auxiliaries *could, should*, and *would* were often used indiscriminately. Again, later in this scene, "*should* not upbraid our course"; *should* for *would.*

[151] *Bat-fowling* was a term used of catching birds in the night. Fielding, in *Joseph Andrews*, calls it *bird-batting*, and says "it is performed by holding a large clap-net before a lantern, and at the same time beating the bushes; for the birds, when they are disturbed from their places of rest or roost, immediately make to the light, and so are enticed within the net.

[152] That is, "hazard my character for discretion, or put it in peril."

[153] "Do not *slight* or *neglect* the *offer of sleep* which it holds out," or "when it offers to make you sleepy." *Heavy* is here used proleptically, or *anticipatively.*

SEBASTIAN. Why
    Doth it not then our eyelids sink? I find not
    Myself disposed to sleep.
ANTONIO. Nor I; my spirits are nimble.
    They fell together all, as by consent;
    They dropp'd, as by a thunder-stroke. What might,
    Worthy Sebastian? O, what might![154]—No more:—
    And yet me thinks I see it in thy face,
    What thou shouldst be: the occasion speaks thee;[155] and
    My strong imagination sees a crown
    Dropping upon thy head.
SEBASTIAN. What, art thou waking?
ANTONIO. Do you not hear me speak?
SEBASTIAN. I do; and surely
    It is a sleepy language and thou speak'st
    Out of thy sleep. What is it thou didst say?
    This is a strange repose, to be asleep
    With eyes wide open; standing, speaking, moving,
    And yet so fast asleep.
ANTONIO. Noble Sebastian,
    Thou let'st thy fortune sleep,—die, rather; wink'st
    Whiles thou art waking.[156]
SEBASTIAN. Thou dost snore distinctly;
    There's meaning in thy snores.
ANTONIO. I am more serious than my custom: you
    Must be so too, if heed me; which to do
    Trebles thee o'er.[157]
SEBASTIAN. Well, I am standing water.[158]
ANTONIO. I'll teach you how to flow.
SEBASTIAN. Do so: to ebb
    Hereditary sloth instructs me.
ANTONIO. O,
    If you but knew how you the purpose cherish
    Whiles thus you mock it! how, in stripping it,
    You more invest it![159] Ebbing men, indeed,

---

[154] "What might *you be*!" is probably the meaning.

[155] Antonio is probably aiming to tempt Sebastian by flattery; declaring that he sees royalty or majesty in his looks, and that the present occasion bespeaks, points out, or proclaims his elevation to the throne.

[156] "Closest thine eyes as if asleep while thou art awake." *While*, *whiles*, and *whilst* were used indifferently.

[157] "The doing of which will make thee thrice what thou art now."

[158] Water standing between ebb and flow, and so ready to be moved in either direction. So in *Twelfth Night*, i. 5: "'Tis with him e'en *standing water* between boy and man."

Most often do so near the bottom run
By their own fear or sloth.
SEBASTIAN. Prithee, say on:
The setting of thine eye and cheek proclaim
A matter from thee, and a birth indeed
Which throes thee much to yield.[160]
ANTONIO. Thus, sir:
Although this lord of weak remembrance, this,
Who shall be of as little memory[161]
When he is earth'd, hath here almost persuade—
For he's a spirit of persuasion, only
Professes to persuade,—the king his son's alive,
'Tis as impossible that he's undrown'd
And he that sleeps here swims.
SEBASTIAN. I have no hope
That he's undrown'd.
ANTONIO. O, out of that 'no hope'
What great hope have you! no hope that way is
Another way so high a hope that even
Ambition cannot pierce a wink beyond,—
But doubt discovery there.[162] Will you grant with me
That Ferdinand is drown'd?
SEBASTIAN. He's gone.
ANTONIO. Then, tell me,
Who's the next heir of Naples?
SEBASTIAN. Claribel.
ANTONIO. She that is queen of Tunis; she that dwells
Ten leagues beyond man's life;[163] she that from Naples
Can have no note,[164] unless the sun were post—
The man i' the moon's too slow—till new-born chins
Be rough and razorable; she that—from whom[165]

---

[159] Sebastian shows that he both takes and welcomes Antonio's suggestion, by his making it a theme of jest; and the more he thus denudes the hint of obscurity by playing with it, the more he clothes it with his own approval.—"*Ebbing* men" are men whose fortunes are ebbing away or declining.

[160] "In the yielding of which you struggle very hard, and suffer much pain."—*Matter*, here, is *something of vast import.*

[161] *Will* be as little remembered, or as quickly forgotten, as he is apt to forget. *Weak remembrance* means *feeble memory.* Francisco is the lord referred to.—*Shall* where present usage requires *will*; the two being often used indiscriminately.

[162] Cannot pierce so much beyond as may be measured by a wink of the eye; *wink* meaning the same as *jot* or *atom.* Probably all are familiar with the word in that sense.—The last clause is obscure, or worse: probably, if the text be right, the force of *cannot* was meant to be continued over *But doubt.*

[163] Beyond a lifetime of travelling. Of course this passage is a piece of intentional hyperbole; and Sebastian shows that he takes it so, by exclaiming, "What *stuff* is this!"

[164] *Note* for *knowledge* or *notice.* Repeatedly so.

We all were sea-swallow'd, though some cast again;[166]
And by that destiny to perform an act
Whereof what's past is prologue, what to come
In yours and my discharge.

SEBASTIAN. What stuff is this! how say you?
'Tis true, my brother's daughter's queen of Tunis;
So is she heir of Naples; 'twixt which regions
There is some space.

ANTONIO. A space whose every cubit
Seems to cry out, *How shall that Claribel*
Measure us back to Naples?[167] *Keep in Tunis,*
And let Sebastian wake! Say, this were death
That now hath seized them; why, they were no worse
Than now they are. There be that can rule Naples
As well as he that sleeps; lords that can prate
As amply and unnecessarily
As this Gonzalo; I myself could make
A chough of as deep chat.[168] O, that you bore
The mind that I do! what a sleep were this
For your advancement! Do you understand me?

SEBASTIAN. Methinks I do.

ANTONIO. And how does your content
Tender your own good fortune?[169]

SEBASTIAN. I remember
You did supplant your brother Prospero.

ANTONIO. True:
And look how well my garments sit upon me;
Much feater[170] than before: my brother's servants
Were then my fellows; now they are my men.

SEBASTIAN. But, for your conscience?

---

[165] *For whom* is here equivalent to *because of whom*, or *on whose account. For* is often used so. Antonio means, apparently, to imply that, inasmuch as Claribel has been the occasion of what has befallen them, they need not scruple to cut her off from the Neapolitan throne. And he goes on to intimate that, by the recent strange events, Sebastian and himself are marked out, as by destiny, for some mighty achievement or some peerless honour.

[166] The image is of being swallowed by the sea, and then cast up, or cast *ashore.*— In the next line, "by that destiny" is by the same destiny through which they have so miraculously escaped drowning.

[167] "Measure the distance back from Naples to us;" or "*return* to us."

[168] Could *produce, breed,* or *train* a parrot to talk as wisely. A *chough* is a bird of the jackdaw kind.

[169] Obscure, again. But the meaning seems to be, "How does your present *contentment*, that is, apathy or indifference, regard or look out for your own advantage or interest?" To *tender* a thing is to *take care of* it, or be *careful for* it.

[170] *Feater* is *more finely*, or more *becomingly.—Fellows*, in the next line, is *equals.* The word is often used in that sense.

ANTONIO. Ay, sir; where lies that? if 'twere a kibe,[171]
'Twould put me to my slipper: but I feel not
This deity in my bosom: twenty consciences,
That stand 'twixt me and Milan, candied[172] be they
And melt ere they molest! Here lies your brother,
No better than the earth he lies upon,
If he were that which now he's like,[173] that's dead;
Whom I, with this obedient steel, three inches of it,
Can lay to bed for ever; whiles you, doing thus,
To the perpetual wink for aye might put
This ancient morsel, this Sir Prudence, who
Should not upbraid our course. For all the rest,
They'll take suggestion[174] as a cat laps milk;
They'll tell[175] the clock to any business that
We say befits the hour.

SEBASTIAN. Thy case, dear friend,
Shall be my precedent; as thou got'st Milan,
I'll come by Naples. Draw thy sword: one stroke
Shall free thee from the tribute which thou payest;
And I the king shall love thee.

ANTONIO. Draw together;
And when I rear my hand, do you the like,
To fall it on Gonzalo.

SEBASTIAN. O, but one word. [*They converse apart.*]

[*Music. Re-enter* ARIEL, *invisible.*]

ARIEL. My master through his art foresees the danger
That you, his friend, are in; and sends me forth—
For else his project dies—to keep them living.

[*Sings in* GONZALO's *ear.*]

---

[171] The Poet has *kibe* several times for the well-known heel-sore, an ulcerated chilblain.

[172] *Candied*, here, is *congealed*, or *crystallized.* So in *Timon of Athens*, iv. 3: "Will the cold brook, *candied with ice*, caudle thy morning taste?"

[173] That is, *dead*; as sleep and death look just like twins.

[174] *Suggest* and its derivatives were often used in the sense of to *tempt.* Thus Shakespeare has such phrases as "tender youth is soon *suggested*" and "what serpent hath *suggested* thee." The meaning of the text is, "They'll fall in with any temptation"; referring to the other lords present.

[175] *Tell*, again, for *count.* The meaning is," They'll speak whatever words we choose to have them speak," or "we put into their mouths."

While you here do snoring lie,
Open-eyed conspiracy
His time doth take.
If of life you keep a care,
Shake off slumber, and beware:
Awake, awake!

ANTONIO. Then let us both be sudden.
GONZALO. [*Waking*.] Now, good angels
Preserve the king.—[*To* SEBASTIAN *and* ANTONIO.] Why, how now? how awake!—[*To* ALONSO.] Ho, awake!—
[*To* SEBASTIAN *and* ANTONIO.] Why are you drawn? wherefore this ghastly looking?
GONZALO. [*Waking*.] What's the matter?
SEBASTIAN. Whiles we stood here securing your repose,
Even now, we heard a hollow burst of bellowing
Like bulls, or rather lions: did't not wake you?
It struck mine ear most terribly.
ALONSO. I heard nothing.
ANTONIO. O, 'twas a din to fright a monster's ear,
To make an earthquake! sure, it was the roar
Of a whole herd of lions.
ALONSO. Heard you this, Gonzalo?
GONZALO. Upon mine honour, sir, I heard a humming,
And that a strange one too, which did awake me:
I shaked you, sir, and cried: as mine eyes open'd,
I saw their weapons drawn: there was a noise,
That's verily. 'Tis best we stand upon our guard,
Or that we quit this place; let's draw our weapons.
ALONSO. Lead off this ground; and let's make further search
For my poor son.
GONZALO. Heavens keep him from these beasts!
For he is, sure, i' the island.
ALONSO. Lead away.

[*Exit with the others*.]

ARIEL. Prospero my lord shall know what I have done:
So, king, go safely on to seek thy son. [*Exit*.]

Scene II.

Another Part of the Island.

[*Enter* CALIBAN *with a burden of wood. A noise of thunder heard.*]

CALIBAN. All the infections that the sun sucks up
From bogs, fens, flats, on Prosper fall and make him
By inch-meal[176] a disease! His spirits hear me
And yet I needs must curse. But they'll nor pinch,
Fright me with urchin-shows,[177] pitch me i' the mire,
Nor lead me, like a firebrand,[178] in the dark
Out of my way, unless he bid 'em; but
For every trifle are they set upon me;
Sometime[179] like apes that mow[180] and chatter at me
And after bite me, then like hedgehogs which
Lie tumbling in my barefoot way and mount
Their pricks[181] at my footfall; sometime am I
All wound with adders who with cloven tongues
Do hiss me into madness. Lo, now, lo!
Here comes a spirit of his, and to torment me
For bringing wood in slowly. I'll fall flat;
Perchance he will not mind me.

[*Enter* TRINCULO.]

TRINCULO. Here's neither bush nor shrub, to bear off any weather at all, and another storm brewing; I hear it sing i' the wind: yond same black cloud, yond huge one, looks like a foul bombard[182] that would shed his liquor. If it should thunder as it did before, I know not where to hide my head: yond same cloud cannot choose but fall by pailfuls.—What have we here? a man or a fish? dead or alive? A fish: he smells like a fish; a very ancient and fish- like smell; a kind of not of the newest poor-john.[183] A strange fish! Were I in

---

[176] *Inch-meal* and *limb-meal* were used just as we use *piece-meal.*

[177] *Urchin-shows* are *fairy-shows*; as *urchin* was the name of a certain description of fairies. See page 34, note 97.

[178] The *ignis fatuus* was thought to be the work of naughty spirits.

[179] *Sometime* and *sometimes* were used indiscriminately.

[180] To *mow* is to *make mouths.* So Nash's *Pierce Penniless*: "Nobody at home but an ape, that sat in the porch, and made mops and *mows* at him."

[181] *Pricks* is the ancient word for *prickles.*

[182] A *bombard* is a black jack of leather, to hold beer, &c.

[183] *Poor-john* is an old name for *hake* salted and dried.

England now, as once I was, and had but this fish painted, not a holiday fool there but would give a piece of silver: there would this monster make a man;[184] any strange beast there makes a man: when they will not give a doit to relieve a lame beggar, they will lazy out ten to see a dead Indian. Legged like a man and his fins like arms! Warm o' my troth! I do now let loose my opinion; hold it no longer: this is no fish, but an islander, that hath lately suffered by a thunderbolt. [*Thunder.*] Alas, the storm is come again! my best way is to creep under his gaberdine;[185] there is no other shelter hereabouts: misery acquaints a man with strange bed-fellows. I will here shroud till the dregs of the storm be past. [*Creeps under* CALIBAN's *garment.*]

[*Enter* STEPHANO, *singing*: *a bottle in his hand.*]

STEPHANO.

I shall no more to sea, to sea,
Here shall I die ashore;—

This is a very scurvy tune to sing at a man's funeral: well, here's my comfort. [*Drinks.*]

[*Sings.*]

The master, the swabber,[186] *the boatswain and I,*
The gunner and his mate
Loved Mall, Meg and Marian and Margery,
But none of us cared for Kate;
For she had a tongue with a tang,[187]
Would cry to a sailor, Go hang!
She loved not the savour of tar nor of pitch;
Yet a tailor might scratch her where'er she did itch:
Then to sea, boys, and let her go hang!

This is a scurvy tune too: but here's my comfort. [*Drinks.*]

---

[184] Sets a man up, or *makes his fortune.* The phrase was often used thus. So in *A Midsummer-Night's Dream*, iv. 2: "If our sport had gone forward, we had all been *made men.*" And in *Othello*, i. 2: "He hath boarded a land carack: if it prove lawful prize, he's *made* for ever."

[185] *A gaberdine* was a coarse outer garment. "A shepherd's pelt, frock, or *gaberdine*, such a coarse long jacket as our porters wear over the rest of their garments," says Cotgrave. "A kind of rough cassock or frock like an Irish mantle," says Philips.

[186] A *swabber* is one whose special business it is to sweep, mop, or *swab* the deck of a ship.

[187] *Tang* was used of what has a pungent or biting taste or flavour.

CALIBAN. Do not torment me:—O!

STEPHANO. What's the matter? Have we devils here? Do you put tricks upon's with savages and men of Inde,[188] ha? I have not scaped drowning to be afeard now of your four legs; for it hath been said, As proper a man as ever went on four legs cannot make him give ground; and it shall be said so again while Stephano breathes at's nostrils.

CALIBAN. The spirit torments me:—O!

STEPHANO. This is some monster of the isle with four legs, who hath got, as I take it, an ague. Where the devil should he learn our language? I will give him some relief, if it be but for that. if I can recover him and keep him tame and get to Naples with him, he's a present for any emperor that ever trod on neat's leather.[189]

CALIBAN. Do not torment me, prithee;
I'll bring my wood home faster.

STEPHANO. He's in his fit now and does not talk after the wisest. He shall taste of my bottle: if he have never drunk wine afore will go near to remove his fit. If I can recover him and keep him tame, I will not take too much for him;[190] he shall pay for him that hath him, and that soundly.

CALIBAN. Thou dost me yet but little hurt;
Thou wilt anon, I know it by thy trembling:
Now Prosper works upon thee.

STEPHANO. Come on your ways; open your mouth; here is that which will give language to you, cat:[191] open your mouth; this will shake your shaking, I can tell you, and that soundly: [*Gives him drink.*] you cannot tell who's your friend: open your chaps again. [*Gives him another drink.*]

TRINCULO. I should know that voice: it should be—but he is drowned; and these are devils:—O, defend me!

STEPHANO. Four legs and two voices,—a most delicate monster! His forward voice now is to speak well of his friend; his backward voice is to utter foul speeches and to detract. If all the wine in my

---

[188] Alluding, probably, to the impostures practised by showmen, who often exhibited sham wonders pretended to be brought from America. *Inde* for *India*, East or West.

[189] *Neat* is an old epithet for all cattle of the bovine genus. So that *neat's-leather* is *cowhide* or *calfskin.* So in *The Winter's Tale*, i. 2: "And yet the steer, the heifer, and the calf are all call'd *neat.*"

[190] A piece of vulgar irony, meaning, "I'll take as much as I can get."

[191] Shakespeare gives his characters appropriate language: "They belch forth proverbs in their drink," "Good liquor will *make a cat speak*" and "He who eats with the devil had need of a *long spoon.*"

bottle will recover him, I will help his ague. [*Gives him drink.*]—Come,—Amen![192] I will pour some in thy other mouth.

TRINCULO. Stephano!

STEPHANO. Doth thy other mouth call me? Mercy, mercy! This is a devil, and no monster: I will leave him; I have no long spoon.

TRINCULO. Stephano!—If thou beest Stephano, touch me and speak to me: for I am Trinculo,—be not afeard,—thy good friend Trinculo.

STEPHANO. If thou beest Trinculo, come forth: I'll pull thee by the lesser legs: if any be Trinculo's legs, these are they. [*Pulls* TRINCULO *out.*] Thou art very Trinculo[193] indeed! How camest thou to be the siege of this moon-calf?[194] can he vent Trinculos?

TRINCULO. I took him to be killed with a thunder-stroke. But art thou not drowned, Stephano? I hope now thou art not drowned. Is the storm overblown? I hid me under the dead moon-calf's gaberdine for fear of the storm. And art thou living, Stephano? O Stephano, two Neapolitans 'scaped!

STEPHANO. Prithee, do not turn me about; my stomach is not constant.

CALIBAN. [*Aside.*] These be fine things, an if[195] they be not sprites. That's a brave god and bears celestial liquor. I will kneel to him.

STEPHANO. How didst thou 'scape? How camest thou hither? swear by this bottle how thou camest hither. I escaped upon a butt of sack which the sailors heaved o'erboard, by this bottle; which I made of the bark of a tree with mine own hands since I was cast ashore.

CALIBAN. I'll swear upon that bottle to be thy true subject; for the liquor is not earthly.

STEPHANO. Here; swear then how thou escapedst.

TRINCULO. Swum ashore. man, like a duck: I can swim like a duck, I'll be sworn.

STEPHANO. Here, kiss the book. [*Gives him drink.*] Though thou canst swim like a duck, thou art made like a goose.

TRINCULO. O Stephano. hast any more of this?

STEPHANO. The whole butt, man: my cellar is in a rock by the sea-side where my wine is hid.—How now, moon-calf! how does thine ague?

CALIBAN. Hast thou not dropp'd from heaven?

---

192 Stephano is frightened, and put to his religion; and *Amen*! is the best he can do towards praying.

193 That is, the *real* or *veritable* Trinculo. The Poet often has *very* so.

194 *Moon-calf* was an imaginary monster, supposed to be generated or misshapen through lunar influence. So in Holland's Pliny: "A false conception called *mola*, that is a moone-calfe; that is to say, a lump of flesh without shape, without life."—*Siege* is an old word for *seat.* So in *Measure for Measure*, iv. 2: "Upon the very *siege* of justice."

195 In old English, *if an*, and *an if are* exactly equivalent expressions; the latter being merely a reduplication; though it sometimes has the force of *even if.*

STEPHANO. Out o' the moon, I do assure thee: I was the man i' the moon when time was.

CALIBAN. I have seen thee in her and I do adore thee:
My mistress show'd me thee and thy dog and thy bush.[196]

STEPHANO. Come, swear to that; kiss the book:
I will furnish it anon with new contents swear. [*Gives* CALIBAN *drink.*]

TRINCULO. By this good light, this is a very shallow monster!—I afeard of him!—a very weak monster!—*The-Man-i'-the-moon*!—A most poor credulous monster!—Well drawn, monster, in good sooth.[197]

CALIBAN. I'll show thee every fertile inch o' th' island;
And I will kiss thy foot: I prithee, be my god.

TRINCULO. By this light, a most perfidious and drunken monster! when his god's asleep, he'll rob his bottle.[198]

CALIBAN. I'll kiss thy foot; I'll swear myself thy subject.

STEPHANO. Come on then; down, and swear.

TRINCULO. I shall laugh myself to death at this puppy-headed monster. A most scurvy monster! I could find in my heart to beat him,—

STEPHANO. Come, kiss. [*Gives* CALIBAN *drink.*]

TRINCULO.—but that the poor monster's in drink: an abominable monster!

CALIBAN. I'll show thee the best springs; I'll pluck thee berries;
I'll fish for thee and get thee wood enough.
A plague upon the tyrant that I serve!
I'll bear him no more sticks, but follow thee,
Thou wondrous man.

TRINCULO. A most ridiculous monster, to make a wonder of a
Poor drunkard!

CALIBAN. I prithee, let me bring thee where crabs grow;
And I with my long nails will dig thee pig-nuts;[199]
Show thee a jay's nest and instruct thee how
To snare the nimble marmoset; I'll bring thee
To clustering filberts and sometimes I'll get thee
Young staniels[200] from the rock. Wilt thou go with me?

---

[196] So in *A Midsummer*, v. 1: "This man, with lantern, dog, and bush of thorn, presenteth moonshine."

[197] *Well drawn* probably means that Caliban has taken a large *draught* of the liquor; as we should say, a *bumper*.—"In good sooth," *sooth* is the same as *truth*. So *soothsayer* originally meant a *truth-speaker*.

[198] That is, will steal the liquor out of his bottle.

[199] *Pig-nuts* are probably much the same as what we call *ground-nuts*,—a small bulbous root growing wild.

[200] The *staniel* is a species of hawk, also called kestil; a "beautiful species," says Montagu.

STEPHANO. I prithee now, lead the way without any more talking.—Trinculo, the king and all our company else being drowned, we will inherit here.[201] Here; bear my bottle: fellow Trinculo, we'll fill him by and by again.

CALIBAN. [*Sings drunkenly.*] Farewell master; farewell, farewell!

TRINCULO. A howling monster: a drunken monster!

CALIBAN. No more dams I'll make for fish
Nor fetch in firing at requiring;
Nor scrape trencher, nor wash dish
'Ban, 'Ban, Ca—Caliban
Has a new master: get a new man.
Freedom, hey-day! hey-day, freedom! freedom, hey-day, freedom!

STEPHANO. O brave monster! lead the way. [*Exeunt.*]

ACT III.

SCENE I.

Before PROSPERO'*s cell.*

[*Enter* FERDINAND, *bearing a log.*]

FERDINAND. There be some sports are painful, and their labour
Delight in them sets off:[202] some kinds of baseness
Are nobly undergone and most poor matters
Point to rich ends. This my mean task
Would be as heavy to me as odious, but
The mistress which I serve quickens what's dead
And makes my labours pleasures: O, she is
Ten times more gentle than her father's crabbed,
And he's composed of harshness. I must remove
Some thousands of these logs and pile them up,
Upon a sore injunction: my sweet mistress
Weeps when she sees me work, and says, such baseness
Had never like executor. I forget:
But these sweet thoughts do even refresh my labours,
Most busy lest, when I do it least.[203]

---

[201] To *possess*, or to *take possession*, is one of the old meanings of to *inherit*; and so the Poet often uses it.

[202] The delight we take in those painful sports *offsets* or *compensates* the exertion they put us to. A similar thought occurs in *Macbeth*: "The labour we delight in physics pain."

[203] That is, "*I being* most busy when I am least occupied." The sense of the two lines appears to be, "The sweet thoughts attending my labour, and springing from what Miranda is thereby moved to say, make even the labour itself refreshing to me; so that I am happiest when I work hardest, and most weary when working least." And Ferdinand

[*Enter* MIRANDA; *and* PROSPERO *behind.*]

MIRANDA. Alas, now, pray you,
Work not so hard: I would the lightning had
Burnt up those logs that you are enjoin'd to pile!
Pray, set it down and rest you: when this burns,
'Twill weep for having wearied you. My father
Is hard at study; pray now, rest yourself;
He's safe for these three hours.
FERDINAND. O most dear mistress,
The sun will set before I shall discharge
What I must strive to do.
MIRANDA. If you'll sit down,
I'll bear your logs the while: pray, give me that;
I'll carry it to the pile.
FERDINAND. No, precious creature;
I had rather crack my sinews, break my back,
Than you should such dishonour undergo,
While I sit lazy by.
MIRANDA. It would become me
As well as it does you: and I should do it
With much more ease; for my good will is to it,
And yours it is against.
PROSPERO. [*Aside.*] Poor worm, thou art infected!
This visitation shows it.
MIRANDA. You look wearily.
FERDINAND. No, noble mistress; 'tis fresh morning with me
When you are by at night. I do beseech you,—
Chiefly that I might set it in my prayers,—
What is your name?
MIRANDA. Miranda:—O my father,
I have broke your hest to say so!
FERDINAND. Admired Miranda!
Indeed the top of admiration! worth
What's dearest to the world! Full many a lady
I have eyed with best regard and many a time
The harmony of their tongues hath into bondage
Brought my too diligent ear: for several virtues
Have I liked several women; never any
With so fun soul, but some defect in her

"forgets" his task, or loses all sense of its irksomeness, in the pleasantness of his thoughts. "And Jacob served seven years for Rachel; and they seemed unto him but a few days, for the love he had to her."

Did quarrel with the noblest grace she owed
And put it to the foil:[204] but you, O you,
So perfect and so peerless, are created
Of every creature's best!

MIRANDA. I do not know
One of my sex; no woman's face remember,
Save, from my glass, mine own; nor have I seen
More that I may call men than you, good friend,
And my dear father: how features are abroad,
I am skilless of; but, by my modesty,
The jewel in my dower, I would not wish
Any companion in the world but you,
Nor can imagination form a shape,
Besides yourself, to like of. But I prattle
Something too wildly and my father's precepts
I therein do forget.

FERDINAND. I am in my condition
A prince, Miranda; I do think, a king;
I would, not so!—and would no more endure
This wooden slavery than to suffer
The flesh-fly blow[205] my mouth. Hear my soul speak:
The very instant that I saw you, did
My heart fly to your service; there resides,
To make me slave to it; and for your sake
Am I this patient log-man.

MIRANDA. Do you love me?

FERDINAND. O Heaven, O Earth, bear witness to this sound
And crown what I profess with kind event
If I speak true! if hollowly, invert
What best is boded me to mischief! I
Beyond all limit of what else[206] i' the world
Do love, prize, honour you.

MIRANDA. I am a fool
To weep at what I am glad of.

PROSPERO. [*Aside.*] Fair encounter
Of two most rare affections! Heavens rain grace
On that which breeds between 'em!

---

[204] I am not quite clear as to the meaning of this. The Poet often uses *foil* for *sword*; and so the sense may be, "put it to the use of its weapon in self-defence." Probably, however, *putting it to the foil* has the sense merely of *foiling it*. To *foil* is to *baffle*, to *frustrate*, to *render nugatory*.

[205] The *flesh-fly* is the fly that *blows* dead flesh, that is, lays maggot-eggs upon it, and so hastens its putrefaction.

[206] "*What* else" for *whatsoever* else. The Poet has many instances of relative pronouns thus used *indefinitely*. So in *King Lear*, v. 3: "*What* in the world he is that names me traitor, villain-like he lies."

FERDINAND. Wherefore weep you?
MIRANDA. At mine unworthiness that dare not offer
What I desire to give, and much less take
What I shall die to want.[207] But this is trifling;
And all the more it seeks to hide itself,
The bigger bulk it shows. Hence, bashful cunning!
And prompt me, plain and holy innocence!
I am your wife, it you will marry me;
If not, I'll die your maid: to be your fellow[208]
You may deny me; but I'll be your servant,
Whether you will or no.
FERDINAND. My mistress, dearest;
And I thus humble ever.
MIRANDA. My husband, then?
FERDINAND. Ay, with a heart as willing
As bondage e'er of freedom:[209] here's my hand.
MIRANDA. And mine, with my heart in't; and now farewell
Till half an hour hence.
FERDINAND. A thousand thousand![210]

[*Exeunt* FERDINAND *and* MIRANDA.]

PROSPERO. So glad of this as they I cannot be,
Who are surprised withal; but my rejoicing
At nothing can be more. I'll to my book,
For yet ere supper-time must I perform
Much business appertaining. [*Exit.*]

SCENE II.

Another Part of the Island.

[*Enter* CALIBAN, STEPHANO, *and* TRINCULO *with a bottle.*]

STEPHANO. Tell not me; when the butt is out, we will drink water; not a drop before: therefore bear up, and board 'em.[211] Servant-monster, drink to me.

---

[207] Die *from wanting*, or *by wanting*. Another gerundial infinitive. We have a like expression in *Much Ado*: "You kill me *to deny* it."

[208] *Fellow* for *companion* or *equal*, as before. See page 49, note 170.

[209] The abstract for the concrete. "I accept you for my wife as willingly as ever a bondman accepted of freedom."

[210] Meaning a thousand thousand *farewells*; this word being taken literally, like the Latin *bene vale*.

[211] "To bear up, put the helm up, and keep a vessel off her course." So says Admiral Smith.

TRINCULO. Servant-monster! the folly of this island! They say there's but five upon this isle: we are three of them; if th' other two be brained like us, the state totters.

STEPHANO. Drink, servant-monster, when I bid thee: thy eyes are almost set[212] in thy head. [CALIBAN *drinks*.]

TRINCULO. Where should they be set else? he were a brave monster indeed, if they were set in his tail.

STEPHANO. My man-monster hath drown'd his tongue in sack: for my part, the sea cannot drown me; I swam, ere I could recover the shore, five and thirty leagues off and on. By this light.—thou shalt be my lieutenant, monster, or my standard.[213]

TRINCULO. Your lieutenant, if you list; he's no standard.[214]

STEPHANO. We'll not run, Monsieur Monster.

TRINCULO. Nor go neither; but you'll lie like dogs and yet say nothing neither.

STEPHANO. Moon-calf, speak once in thy life, if thou beest a good moon-calf.

CALIBAN. How does thy honour? Let me lick thy shoe.
I'll not serve him; he's not valiant.

TRINCULO. Thou liest, most ignorant monster: I am in case to jostle a constable.[215] Why, thou debosh'd[216] fish thou, was there ever man a coward that hath drunk so much sack as I to-day? Wilt thou tell a monstrous lie, being but half a fish and half a monster?

CALIBAN. Lo, how he mocks me! wilt thou let him, my lord?

TRINCULO. *Lord*, quoth he! That a monster should be such a natural![217]

CALIBAN. Lo, lo, again! bite him to death, I prithee.

STEPHANO. Trinculo, keep a good tongue in your head: if you prove a mutineer,—the next tree! The poor monster's my subject and he shall not suffer indignity.

CALIBAN. I thank my noble lord. Wilt thou be pleased to hearken once again to the suit I made to thee?

STEPHANO. Marry, will I kneel and repeat it; I will stand, and so shall Trinculo.

---

212 *Set* here means, I suppose, fixed in a vacant stare. So in *Twelfth Night*, v. 1: "He's drunk, Sir Toby, an hour agone; his *eyes were set* at eight i' the morning."

213 *Standard*, like *ensign*, is put for the *bearer* of a standard.

214 Trinculo is punning upon *standard*, and probably means that Caliban is too drunk to *stand*.

215 The jester is breaking jests upon himself; his meaning being, "One so deep in drink as I am is valiant enough to quarrel with an officer of the law."

216 *Debosh'd* is an old form of *debauched*. Cotgrave explains, "Deboshed, lewd, incontinent, ungracious, dissolute, naught."

217 *Natural* was used for *simpleton* or *fool*. There is also a quibble intended between *monster* and *natural*, a monster being *unnatural*.

[*Enter* ARIEL, *invisible.*]

CALIBAN. As I told thee before, I am subject to a tyrant, a sorcerer, that by his cunning hath cheated me of the island.

ARIEL. Thou liest.

CALIBAN. [*To* TRINCULO.] Thou liest, thou jesting monkey, thou:
I would my valiant master would destroy thee!
I do not lie.

STEPHANO. Trinculo, if you trouble him any more in's tale, by this hand, I will supplant some of your teeth.

TRINCULO. Why, I said nothing.

STEPHANO. Mum, then, and no more.—[*To* CALIBAN.] Proceed.

CALIBAN. I say, by sorcery he got this isle;
From me he got it. if thy greatness will
Revenge it on him,—for I know thou darest,
But this thing dare not,—

STEPHANO. That's most certain.

CALIBAN.—Thou shalt be lord of it and I'll serve thee.

STEPHANO. How now shall this be compassed?
Canst thou bring me to the party?

CALIBAN. Yea, yea, my lord: I'll yield him thee asleep,
Where thou mayst knock a nail into his bead.

ARIEL. Thou liest; thou canst not.

CALIBAN. What a pied ninny's this![218]—Thou scurvy patch!—
I do beseech thy greatness, give him blows
And take his bottle from him: when that's gone
He shall drink nought but brine; for I'll not show him
Where the quick freshes[219] are.

STEPHANO. Trinculo, run into no further danger: interrupt the monster one word further, and, by this hand, I'll turn my mercy out o' doors and make a stock-fish[220] of thee.

TRINCULO. Why, what did I? I did nothing. I'll go farther off.

STEPHANO. Didst thou not say he lied?

ARIEL. Thou liest.

STEPHANO. Do I so? take thou that. [*Strikes him.*] As you like this, give me the lie another time.

TRINCULO. I did not give the lie. Out o' your wits and bearing too? A pox o' your bottle! this can sack and drinking do. A murrain on your monster, and the devil take your fingers!

---

[218] *Pied* is *dappled* or *diversely-coloured.* Trinculo is "an allowed Fool" or jester, and wears a motley dress. *Patch* refers to the same circumstance.

[219] *Quick freshes* are living springs of fresh water.

[220] A *stock-fish* appears to have been a thing for practising upon with the fist, or with a cudgel. Ben Jonson has it in *Every Man in his Humour*, iii. 2: "'Slight, peace! thou wilt be beaten like a *stock-fishy*."

CALIBAN. Ha, ha, ha!
STEPHANO. Now, forward with your tale.—Prithee, stand farther off.
CALIBAN. Beat him enough: after a little time
I'll beat him too.
STEPHANO. Stand farther.—Come, proceed.
CALIBAN. Why, as I told thee, 'tis a custom with him,
I' th' afternoon to sleep: there thou mayst brain him,[221]
Having first seized his books, or with a log
Batter his skull, or paunch him with a stake,
Or cut his wezand[222] with thy knife. Remember
First to possess his books; for without them
He's but a sot,[223] as I am, nor hath not
One spirit to command: they all do hate him
As rootedly as I. Burn but his books.
He has brave utensils,[224]—for so he calls them,—
Which when he has a house, he'll deck withal
And that most deeply to consider is
The beauty of his daughter; he himself
Calls her a nonpareil: I never saw a woman,
But only Sycorax my dam and she;
But she as far surpasseth Sycorax
As great'st does least.
STEPHANO. Is it so brave a lass?
CALIBAN. Ay, lord; she will become thy bed, I warrant.
And bring thee forth brave brood.
STEPHANO. Monster, I will kill this man: his daughter and I will be king and queen—save our Graces!—and Trinculo and thyself shall be viceroys.—Dost thou like the plot, Trinculo?
TRINCULO. Excellent.
STEPHANO. Give me thy hand: I am sorry I beat thee; but, while thou livest, keep a good tongue in thy head.
CALIBAN. Within this half hour will he be asleep:
Wilt thou destroy him then?
STEPHANO. Ay, on mine honour.

---

[221] That is, knock out his brains. So, in *I Henry the Fourth*, ii. 3, Hotspur says, "Zounds! an I were now by this rascal, I could *brain* him with his lady's fan."

[222] *Weazand* is *windpipe* or *throat*. So Spencer has *weazand-pipe*.

[223] *Sot*, from the French, was frequently used for *fool*; as our word *besotted* sometimes is. The Poet has it repeatedly so.

[224] Here *utensils* has the accent on the first and third syllables. Such, it seems, is the English pronunciation of the word. So Wordsworth has it; and so Milton, in *Paradise Regained*, iii. 336:

> Mules after these, camels, and dromedaries,
> And wagons, fraught with *utensils* of war.

ARIEL. This will I tell my master.

CALIBAN. Thou makest me merry; I am full of pleasure:
Let us be jocund: will you troll the catch
You taught me but while-ere?[225]

STEPHANO. At thy request, monster, I will do reason,[226] any reason. Come on, Trinculo, let us sing.

[*Sings*.] *Flout 'em and scout 'em, And scout 'em and flout 'em;*
Thought is free.

CALIBAN. That's not the tune. [*Ariel plays the tune on a tabor and pipe*.]

STEPHANO. What is this same?

TRINCULO. This is the tune of our catch, played by the picture of Nobody.[227]

STEPHANO. If thou beest a man, show thyself in thy likeness: if thou beest a devil,—take't as thou list.[228]

TRINCULO. O, forgive me my sins!

STEPHANO. He that dies pays all debts: I defy thee.—Mercy upon us!

CALIBAN. Art thou afeard?

STEPHANO. No, monster, not I.

CALIBAN. Be not afeard; the isle is full of noises,
Sounds and sweet airs, that give delight and hurt not.
Sometimes a thousand twangling instruments
Will hum about mine ears, and sometime voices
That, if I then had waked after long sleep,
Will make me sleep again: and then, in dreaming,
The clouds methought would open and show riches
Ready to drop upon me that, when I waked,
I cried to dream again.

STEPHANO. This will prove a brave kingdom to me, where I shall have my music for nothing.

CALIBAN. When Prospero is destroyed.

STEPHANO. That shall be by and by: I remember the story.

---

[225] *While-ere* is *awhile since*. Milton has another form of it in the opening of *Paradise Regained*: "I who *erewhile* the happy garden sung," &c.—A *catch* is a song in parts, where all the singers sing the same notes, but in such order as to make harmony, and where each in turn *catches* the others; sometimes called a *round*.—To *troll* is to *roll* or *round out* glibly or volubly.

[226] That is, will do what is *reasonable*.

[227] *The picture of Nobody* was a common sign, and consisted of a head upon two legs, with arms. There was also a wood-cut prefixed to an old play of *Nobody and Somebody*, which presented this personage.

[228] Here Stephano probably shakes his fist at the invisible musician, or the supposed devil, by way of defiance or bravado.

TRINCULO. The sound is going away; let's follow it, and after do our work.

STEPHANO. Lead, monster; we'll follow.—I would I could see this taborer![229] he lays it on.—Wilt come?

TRINCULO. I'll follow, Stephano. [*Exeunt.*]

SCENE III.

Another Part of the Island.

[*Enter* ALONSO, SEBASTIAN, ANTONIO, GONZALO, ADRIAN, FRANCISCO, *and others.*]

GONZALO. By'r lakin,[230] I can go no further, sir;
My old bones ache: here's a maze trod indeed
Through forth-rights and meanders![231] By your patience,
I needs must rest me.

ALONSO. Old lord, I cannot blame thee,
Who am myself attach'd with weariness,
To the dulling of my spirits: sit down, and rest.
Even here I will put off my hope and keep it
No longer for my flatterer: he is drown'd
Whom thus we stray to find, and the sea mocks
Our frustrate[232] search on land. Well, let him go.

ANTONIO. [*Aside to* SEBASTIAN.] I am right glad that he's so out of hope.
Do not, for one repulse, forego the purpose
That you resolved to effect.

SEBASTIAN. [*Aside to* ANTONIO.] The next advantage
Will we take throughly.[233]

---

229 "You shall heare in the ayre the sound of *tabers and other instruments*, to put the travellers in feare, by evill spirites that makes these soundes, and also do call divers of the travellers by their names." *Travels of Marcus Paulus*, 1579. To some of these Milton also alludes in *Comus*:

> Of calling shapes, and beckoning shadows dire;
> And aery tongues that syllable men's names
> On sands, and shores, and desert wildernesses.

230 *By'r lakin* is a contraction of *by our ladykin*, which, again, is a diminutive of *our Lady*. A softened form of swearing by the Blessed Virgin.

231 *Forth-rights* are straight lines; *meanders*, crooked ones.

232 *Frustrate* for *frustrated*, meaning *baffled*; in accordance with the usage remarked in note 61, page 27. Shakespeare has many preterite forms made in the same way, such as *confiscate*, *consecrate*, *articulate*, and *suffocate*. The usage still holds in a few words, as in *situate*.

ANTONIO. [*Aside to* SEBASTIAN.] Let it be to-night;
For, now they are oppress'd with travel, they
Will not, nor cannot, use such vigilance
As when they are fresh.
SEBASTIAN. [*Aside to* ANTONIO.] I say, to-night: no more.

[*Solemn and strange music.*]

ALONSO. What harmony is this? My good friends, hark!
GONZALO. Marvellous sweet music!

[*Enter* PROSPERO *above, invisible. Enter, below, several strange Shapes, bringing in a banquet; they dance about it with gentle actions of salutation; and, inviting the* KING, *&c., to eat, they depart.*]

ALONSO. Give us kind keepers, Heavens!—What were these?
SEBASTIAN. A living drollery.[234] Now I will believe
That there are unicorns, that in Arabia
There is one tree, the phœnix' throne,[235] one phoenix
At this hour reigning there.
ANTONIO. I'll believe both;
And what does else want credit, come to me,
And I'll be sworn 'tis true: travellers ne'er did lie,
Though fools at home condemn 'em.
GONZALO. If in Naples
I should report this now, would they believe me?
If I should say, I saw such islanders,—
For, certes,[236] these are people of the island,—
Who, though they are of monstrous shape, yet, note,
Their manners are more gentle-kind than of
Our human generation you shall find
Many, nay, almost any.

---

[233] *Through* and *thorough*, *throughly* and *thoroughly*, are but different forms of the same word, as to be *thorough* in a thing is to *go through* it. The old writers use the two forms indifferently. So in St. Matthew, iii. 12: "He will *throughly* purge his floor."

[234] Shows, called *Drolleries*, were in Shakespeare's time performed by puppets only. "A living drollery" is therefore a drollery performed not by puppets but by living personages; a *live puppet-show*.

[235] This imaginary bird is often referred to by the old poets; by Shakespeare repeatedly. The ancient belief is expressed by Lyly in his *Euphues*, thus: "For as there is but one Phœnix in the world, so there is but one tree in Arabia, wherein she buildeth." Also in Holland's Pliny: "I myself have heard strange things of this kind of tree; namely, in regard of the bird Phoenix; for it was assured unto me, that the said bird died with that tree, and revived of itself as the tree sprung again."

[236] *Certes* for *certainly*; used several times by Shakespeare.

PROSPERO. [*Aside.*] Honest lord,
Thou hast said well; for some of you there present
Are worse than devils.
ALONSO. I cannot too much muse[237]
Such shapes, such gesture and such sound, expressing,
Although they want the use of tongue, a kind
Of excellent dumb discourse.
PROSPERO. [*Aside.*] Praise in departing.[238]
FRANCISCO. They vanish'd strangely.
SEBASTIAN. No matter, since
They have left their viands behind; for we have stomachs.
Will't please you taste of what is here?
ALONSO. Not I.
GONZALO. Faith, sir, you need not fear. When we were boys,
Who would believe that there were mountaineers
Dew-lapp'd like bulls, whose throats had hanging at 'em
Wallets of flesh?[239] or that there were such men
Whose heads stood in their breasts?[240] which now we find
Each putter-out of one for five[241] will bring us
Good warrant of.
ALONSO. I will stand to and feed,
Although my last: no matter, since I feel
The best is past.—Brother, my lord the duke,
Stand to and do as we.

[*Thunder and lightning. Enter* ARIEL, *like a harpy*; *claps his wings upon the table*; *and, with a quaint device, the banquet vanishes*.]

ARIEL. You are three men of sin, whom Destiny—

---

[237] To *muse* is to *wonder*; to *wonder at*, in this instance.

[238] "Praise in departing" is said to have been a proverbial phrase, meaning, praise not your entertainment too soon; wait till the end.

[239] In the Alpine and other mountainous regions are many well-known cases of *goitre* that answer to this description. Probably, in the Poet's time, some such had been seen by travellers, but not understood.

[240] These were probably the same that Othello speaks of: "The Anthropophagi, and men whose heads do grow beneath their shoulders." Also in Holland's Pliny: "The Blemmyi, by report, have no heads, but mouth and eyes both in their breast."

[241] A sort of inverted life-insurance was practised by travellers in Shakespeare's time. Before going abroad they *put out* a sum of money, for which they were to receive two, three, four, or even five times the amount upon their return; the rate being according to the supposed danger of the expedition. Of course the sum put out fell to the depositary, in case the *putterout* did not return. So in Ben Jonson's *Every Man out of his Humour*, ii. 1: "I am determined to put forth some five thousand pound, to be paid me five for one, upon the return of myself and wife, and my dog, from the Turk's Court in Constantinople."

That hath to[242] instrument this lower world
And what is in't, the never-surfeited sea
Hath caused to belch up you; and on this island
Where man doth not inhabit; you 'mongst men
Being most unfit to live. I have made you mad;
And even with such-like valour men hang and drown
Their proper selves.

[ALONSO, SEBASTIAN *&c., draw their swords.*]

You fools! I and my fellows
Are ministers of Fate: the elements,
Of whom your swords are temper'd, may as well
Wound the loud winds, or with bemock'd-at stabs
Kill the still-closing waters,[243] as diminish
One dowle[244] that's in my plume: my fellow-ministers
Are like invulnerable. If you could hurt,
Your swords are now too massy for your strengths
And will not be uplifted. But remember—
For that's my business to you—that you three
From Milan did supplant good Prospero;
Exposed unto the sea, which hath requit it,[245]
Him and his innocent child: for which foul deed
The powers, delaying, not forgetting, have
Incensed the seas and shores, yea, all the creatures,
Against your peace. Thee of thy son, Alonso,
They have bereft; and do pronounce by me:
Lingering perdition—worse than any death
Can be at once—shall step by step attend
You and your ways; whose wraths to guard you from,—
Which here, in this most desolate isle, else falls
Upon your heads—is nothing but heart-sorrow
And a clear life ensuing.[246]

[*He vanishes in thunder; then, to soft music enter the Shapes again, and dance, with mocks and mows, and carrying out the table.*]

---

[242] *To*, again, with the force of *for* or *as*. See page 42, note 129.

[243] Waters that *continually* close over cuts made in them, and leave no trace thereof. See page 30, note 79.

[244] *Dowle* and *down* are said to have been equivalent. Here *dowle* seems rather to mean a single particle or thread of downe.

[245] *Requit* for *requited*, like others noted before. See page 27, note 61.

[246] "From whose wrath nothing can shield or deliver you but heart-felt repentance and an amended life, or doing works meet for repentance." *Whose* refers to *powers*, in the sixth line before.

PROSPERO. [*Aside*.] Bravely the figure of this harpy hast thou
Perform'd, my Ariel; a grace it had, devouring:
Of my instruction hast thou nothing bated
In what thou hadst to say: so, with good life
And observation strange,[247] my meaner ministers
Their several kinds have done.[248] My high charms work
And these mine enemies are all knit up
In their distractions; they now are in my power;
And in these fits I leave them, while I visit
Young Ferdinand, whom they suppose is drown'd,
And his and mine loved darling. [*Exit from above*.]
GONZALO. I' the name of something holy, sir, why stand you
In this strange stare?
ALONSO. O, it is monstrous, monstrous:
Methought the billows spoke and told me of it;
The winds did sing it to me, and the thunder,
That deep and dreadful organ-pipe, pronounced
The name of Prosper: it did bass my trespass.
Therefore my son i' the ooze is bedded, and
I'll seek him deeper than e'er plummet sounded
And with him there lie mudded. [*Exit*.]
SEBASTIAN. But one fiend at a time,
I'll fight their legions o'er.
ANTONIO. I'll be thy second.

[*Exeunt* SEBASTIAN, *and* ANTONIO.]

GONZALO. All three of them are desperate: their great guilt,
Like poison given to work a great time after,[249]
Now 'gins to bite the spirits. I do beseech you
That are of suppler joints, follow them swiftly
And hinder them from what this ecstasy[250]
May now provoke them to.
ADRIAN. Follow, I pray you. [*Exeunt*.]

---

[247] The sense appears to be, "with all the truth of life itself, and with rare observance of the proprieties of action."

[248] To do one's *kind* is to act out one's *nature*, or act *according* to one's nature; though in this case the nature is an assumed one, that is, a *part*. So, in *Antony and Cleopatra*, the rustic, speaking of the asp, says, "the worm will *do his kind*." Also in the phrase, "The cat will after *kind*."

[249] The natives of Africa have been supposed to possess the secret how to temper poisons with such art as not to operate till several years after they were administered.

[250] Shakespeare uses *ecstasy* for any alienation of mind, a fit, or madness.

ACT IV.

SCENE I.

Before PROSPERO'*s Cell.*

[*Enter* PROSPERO, FERDINAND, *and* MIRANDA.]

PROSPERO. If I have too austerely punish'd you,
Your compensation[251] makes amends, for I
Have given you here a third of mine own life,[252]
Or that for which I live; who once again
I tender to thy hand: all thy vexations
Were but my trials of thy love and thou
Hast strangely stood the test here, afore Heaven,
I ratify this my rich gift. O Ferdinand,
Do not smile at me that I boast her off,
For thou shalt find she will outstrip all praise
And make it halt behind her.
FERDINAND. I do believe it
Against an oracle.
PROSPERO. Then, as my gift and thine own acquisition
Worthily purchased take my daughter: but
If thou dost break her virgin-knot[253] before
All sanctimonious[254] ceremonies may
With full and holy rite be minister'd,
No sweet aspersion[255] shall the heavens let fall
To make this contract grow: but barren hate,
Sour-eyed disdain and discord shall bestrew
The union of your bed with weeds so loathly[256]
That you shall hate it both: therefore take heed,
As Hymen's lamps shall light you.
FERDINAND. As I hope

---

[251] *Your compensation* is the compensation *you receive.* Shakespeare has many instances of like construction.

[252] "Thread of mine own life" probably means about the same as "my very *heart-strings*"; strings the breaking of which spills the life.

[253] Alluding, no doubt, to the zone or sacred girdle which the old Romans used as the symbol and safeguard of maiden honour.

[254] *Sanctimonious*, here, is *sacred* or *religious.* The marriage *ritual* was supposed to have something of consecrating virtue in it.

[255] *Aspersion* in its primitive sense of *sprinkling*, as with genial rain or dew.—Here, again, as also just after, *shall* for *will.*

[256] Not with wholesome flowers, such as the bridal bed was wont to be decked with, but with *loathsome* weeds.

For quiet days, fair issue and long life,
With such love as 'tis now, the murkiest den,
The most opportune place, the strong'st suggestion[257]
Our worser genius[258] can, shall never melt
Mine honour into lust, to take away
The edge of that day's celebration
When I shall think: or Phoebus' steeds are founder'd,
Or Night kept chain'd below.

PROSPERO. Fairly spoke.
Sit then and talk with her; she is thine own.—
What, Ariel! my industrious servant, Ariel!

[*Enter* ARIEL.]

ARIEL. What would my potent master? here I am.

PROSPERO. Thou and thy meaner fellows your last service
Did worthily perform; and I must use you
In such another trick. Go bring the rabble,
O'er whom I give thee power, here to this place:
Incite them to quick motion; for I must
Bestow upon the eyes of this young couple
Some vanity[259] of mine art: it is my promise,
And they expect it from me.

ARIEL. Presently?

PROSPERO. Ay, with a twink.

ARIEL. Before you can say *Come* and *Go*,
And breathe twice and cry *So, so*,
Each one, tripping on his toe,
Will be here with mop and mow.[260]
Do you love me, master?—no?

PROSPERO. Dearly my delicate Ariel. Do not approach
Till thou dost hear me call.

ARIEL. Well, I conceive. [*Exit*.]

---

[257] *Suggestion*, again, for *temptation*. See page 50, note 174.

[258] *Genius*, *spirit*, and *angel* were used indifferently for what we should call a man's worser or better *self*. *The Edinburgh Review*, July, 1869, has the following: "In mediaeval theology, the rational soul is an angel, the lowest in the hierarchy for being clothed for a time in the perishing vesture of the body. But it is not necessarily an angel of light. It may be a good or evil genius, a guardian angel or a fallen spirit, a demon of light or darkness." See, also, *Julius Cæsar*, ii. 1.

[259] Perhaps meaning some magical show or illusion. *Display*?

[260] *Mop* and *mow* were very often used thus together. To *mow* is to *make mouths*, to *grimace*. Wedgwood, in his *English Etymology*, says that *mop* has exactly the same derivation as *mock*, and means to *gibber*. Thus the ape both *mops* and *mows*; that is, he *gibbers* or *chatters*, and *makes faces*.

PROSPERO. [*To* FERDINAND.] Look thou be true; do not give dalliance
Too much the rein: the strongest oaths are straw
To the fire i' the blood: be more abstemious,
Or else, good night your vow!
FERDINAND. I warrant you sir;
The white cold virgin snow upon my heart
Abates the ardour of my liver.[261]
PROSPERO. Well.
Now come, my Ariel! bring a corollary,[262]
Rather than want a spirit: appear and pertly!
No tongue! all eyes! be silent. [*Soft music.*]

[*Enter* IRIS.]

IRIS. Ceres, most bounteous lady, thy rich leas
Of wheat, rye, barley, vetches, oats and peas;
Thy turfy mountains, where live nibbling sheep,
And flat meads thatch'd with stover,[263] them to keep;
Thy banks with peonied and twilled brims,[264]
Which spongy April[265] at thy hest betrims,
To make cold nymphs chaste crowns; and thy broom -groves,
Whose shadow the dismissed bachelor loves,
Being lass-lorn: thy pole-clipt vineyard;[266]

---

[261] The *liver* was supposed to be the special seat of certain passions, and so was often put for the passions themselves.

[262] *Corollary* here means a surplus number; more than enough.—*Pertly*, in the next line, is *nimbly, alertly.*

[263] *Stover* is fodder and provision of all sorts for cattle. Steevens says that in some counties it "signifies hay made of coarse rank grass, such as even cows will not eat while it is green."

[264] A writer in *The Edinburgh Review* for October, 1872, argues, and, I think, proves, that *peonéd* here refers to the *marsh-marigold*, which grew abundantly on the flat marshy banks of such still-running streams as the Warwickshire Avon, and which was provincially called *peony* or *piony*. He thus compares it with the garden peony: "The flowers, though differing in colour, have a remarkable similarity in general growth and shape, especially in the early stage, when the fully-formed bud is ripe for blowing."—In explanation of *twillèd* the same writer has the following: "*Twills* is given by Halliwell as an old provincial word for *reeds*; and it was applied, like *quills*, to the serried rustling sedges of river reaches and marshy levels. It was indeed while watching the masses of waving sedge cutting the waterline of the Avon, not far from Stratford church, that we first felt the peculiar force and significance of the epithet."

[265] April has the epithet *spongy*, probably because at that season the earth or the air *sponges* up so much water. So, in *Cymbeline*, iv. 2, we have "the *spongy* south," referring to the south or south-west *wind*, which, in England, is apt to be densely charged with moisture; that is, *foggy*; elsewhere called "the foggy south."

[266] *Lass-lorn* is *forsaken by his lass*, the sweet-heart that has *dismissed* him.—*Pole-clipt* probably means poles embraced or clasped by the vines. *Clip* was often used for

And thy sea-marge, sterile and rocky-hard,
Where thou thyself dost air;—the queen o' the sky,
Whose watery arch and messenger am I,
Bids thee leave these, and with her sovereign Grace,
Here on this grass-plot, in this very place,
To come and sport: her peacocks fly amain:
Approach, rich Ceres, her to entertain.

[*Enter* CERES.]

CERES. Hail, many-colour'd messenger, that ne'er
Dost disobey the wife of Jupiter;
Who with thy saffron wings upon my flowers
Diffusest honey-drops, refreshing showers,
And with each end of thy blue bow dost crown
My bosky acres[267] and my unshrubb'd down,
Rich scarf to my proud earth; why hath thy queen
Summon'd me hither, to this short-grass'd green?
IRIS. A contract of true love to celebrate;
And some donation freely to estate
On the blest lovers.
CERES. Tell me, heavenly bow,
If Venus or her son, as thou dost know,
Do now attend the queen? Since they did plot
The means that dusky Dis my daughter got,[268]
Her and her blind boy's scandal'd company
I have forsworn.
IRIS. Of her society
Be not afraid: I met her deity
Cutting the clouds towards Paphos,[269] and her son
Dove-drawn with her. Here thought they to have done
Some wanton charm upon this man and maid,
Whose vows are, that no bed-right shall be paid

---

embrace. So in *Coriolanus*, i. 6: "Let me *clip* ye in arms as sound as when I woo'd."—*Vineyard* is here a trisyllable.

[267] "*Bosky* acres" are *woody* acres, fields intersected by luxuriant hedgerows and copses. So in Milton's *Comus*:

> I know each lane, and every alley green,
> Dingle, or bushy dell of this wild wood,
> And every *bosky* bourn from side to side.

[268] The means whereby Pluto caught and carried of Proserpina. Proserpina was the daughter of Jupiter and Ceres: Dis, King of *dusky* Hades, fell so deep in love with her, that he must needs seize her, *vi et armis*, and spirit her away to Hades, to be his Queen.

[269] A city in Cyprus, where Venus had a favourite country-seat.

Till Hymen's torch be lighted: but vain;
Mars's hot minion is returned again;[270]
Her waspish-headed son has broke his arrows,
Swears he will shoot no more but play with sparrows
And be a boy right out.

CERES. High'st Queen of state,[271]
Great Juno, comes; I know her by her gait.[272]

[*Enter* JUNO.]

JUNO. How does my bounteous sister? Go with me
To bless this twain, that they may prosperous be
And honour'd in their issue.

SONG.

JUNO.

Honour, riches, marriage-blessing,
Long continuance, and increasing,
Hourly joys be still upon you!
Juno sings her blessings upon you.

CERES.

Earth's increase, foison plenty,[273]
Barns and garners never empty,
Vines and clustering bunches growing,
Plants with goodly burthen bowing;
Spring come to you at the farthest
In the very end of harvest![274]

---

[270] Has gone back to Paphos. *Minion* is *darling* or *favourite*, and refers to *Venus.*—In what follows the meaning is, that Cupid is so chagrined and mortified at being thus baffled, that he is determined to give up his business, and act the love-god no more, but be a mere boy, or a boy *outright.*

[271] "High'st Queen of state" is the same as Queen of highest state, or Queen above all other queens. *State* for *throne*, or *chair* of state. So the word was often used.—The Poet has many similar inversions.

[272] Juno was distinguished by her *walk*, as the gods and goddesses generally were. So in *Pericles*, v. 1: "In *pace* another Juno."

[273] "*Foison plenty*" is, strictly speaking, redundant or tautological, as both words mean the same. But *plenty* is used as an adjective,—*plentiful* or *overflowing.* See page 45, note 144.

[274] "May your new Spring come, at the latest, as soon as the harvest of the old one is over!" This explanation is sustained, as Staunton points out, by Amos, ix. 13: "Behold, the days come, saith the Lord, that the ploughman shall overtake the reaper, and the treader of grapes him that soweth the seed." Also, in *The Faerie Queen*, iii. 6, 42:

Scarcity and want shall shun you;
Ceres' blessing so is on you.

FERDINAND. This is a most majestic vision, and
Harmoniously charmingly.[275] May I be bold
To think these spirits?
PROSPERO. Spirits, which by mine art
I have from their confines call'd to enact
My present fancies.
FERDINAND. Let me live here ever;
So rare a wonder'd father[276] and a wife
Makes this place Paradise.

[JUNO *and* CERES *whisper, and send* IRIS *on employment.*]

PROSPERO. Sweet, now, silence!
Juno and Ceres whisper seriously;
There's something else to do: hush, and be mute,
Or else our spell is marr'd.[277]
IRIS. You nymphs, call'd Naiads, of the windring brooks,
With your sedged crowns and ever-harmless looks,
Leave your crisp channels,[278] and on this green land
Answer your summons; Juno does command:
Come, temperate nymphs, and help to celebrate
A contract of true love; be not too late.—

[*Enter certain* NYMPHS.]

There is continuall Spring, and harvest there
Continuall, both meeting in one time.

[275] That is, charmingly harmonious. See note 21, above.—"*So* bold *as* to think." See page 25, note 47.

[276] "So rare-wonder'd a father" is the prose order of the words. The Poet has several such inversions for metre's sake. So in *King John*, iv. 1: "For putting on so new a fashion'd robe." So new-fashion'd a robe. The meaning in the text is, so *rarely-wonderful* a father; and the force of "so rare a *wonder'd*" extends over *wife.* Shakespeare has many instances of the ending *-ed* used in the same way; as in *Macbeth*, iii. 4: "You have broke the good meeting with most *admired* disorder." *Admired* for *admirable*, and in the sense of *wonderful.*

[277] It was supposed that any noise or disturbance would upset or disconcert "the might of magic spells."

[278] *Crisp* is *curled*, from the curl made by a breeze on the surface of the water. The transference of an epithet to an associated object, as of *crisp* from the water to the channel in this instance, is one of Shakespeare's favourite traits of style. So in *Romeo and Juliet*, iii. 5, when the lovers see tokens of the dawn that is to *sever* them, Romeo says, "what envious streaks do lace the *severing clouds* in yonder east."

You sunburnt sicklemen, of August weary,
Come hither from the furrow and be merry:
Make holiday; your rye-straw hats put on
And these fresh nymphs encounter every one
In country footing.

[*Enter certain* REAPERS, *properly habited: they join with the* NYMPHS *in a graceful dance; towards the end whereof* PROSPERO *starts suddenly, and speaks; after which, to a strange, hollow, and confused noise, they heavily vanish.*]

PROSPERO. [*Aside.*] I had forgot that foul conspiracy
Of the beast Caliban and his confederates
Against my life: the minute of their plot
Is almost come.—[*To the* SPIRITS.] Well done! avoid;[279] no more!
FERDINAND. [*To* MIRANDA.] This is strange: your father's in some passion
That works him strongly.
MIRANDA. Never till this day
Saw I him touch'd with anger so distemper'd.
PROSPERO. You do look, my son, in a moved sort,[280]
As if you were dismay'd: be cheerful, sir.
Our revels now are ended. These our actors,
As I foretold you, were all spirits and
Are melted into air, into thin air:
And, like the baseless fabric of this vision,
The cloud-capp'd towers, the gorgeous palaces,
The solemn temples, the great globe itself,
Ye all which it inherit,[281] shall dissolve
And, like this insubstantial pageant faded,[282]
Leave not a rack[283] behind. We are such stuff
As dreams are made on, and our little life
Is rounded with a sleep.[284] Sir, I am vex'd;

---

[279] *Vacate* or *make void* the place; that is to say, *be gone.*

[280] Here, as often, *sort* is *manner* or *way.* So in *Coriolanus*, i. 3: "I pray you, daughter, express yourself in a more comfortable *sort.*"

[281] All who *possess* it. So in the divine beatitude, "Blessed are the meek; for they shall *inherit* the earth." See page 57, note 201.

[282] *Faded*, from the Latin *vado*, is the same as *vanished.*

[283] *Rack* was used of the highest, and therefore lightest or thinnest clouds. So in Bacon's *Silva Silvarum*: "The winds in the upper region (which move the *clouds* above, which we call the *rack*, and are not perceived below) pass without noise."—The word *rack* is from *reek*, that is, *vapour* or *smoke.*

[284] *On* for *of.* Still used so, especially in colloquial speech.—*Rounded* is *finished, rounded off.* The sleep here meant is the sleep of death; as in Hamlet's soliloquy: "To die, to sleep; no more."

Bear with my weakness; my, brain is troubled:
Be not disturb'd with my infirmity:
If you be pleased, retire into my cell
And there repose: a turn or two I'll walk,
To still my beating mind.

FERDINAND *and* MIRANDA. We wish your peace.

PROSPERO. Come with a thought!—I thank ye.[285] [*Exeunt* FERDINAND and MIRANDA.]—Ariel, come!

[*Re-enter* ARIEL.]

ARIEL. Thy thoughts I cleave to. What's thy pleasure?

PROSPERO. Spirit,
We must prepare to meet with[286] Caliban.

ARIEL. Ay, my commander: when I presented Ceres,
I thought to have told thee of it, but I fear'd
Lest I might anger thee.

PROSPERO. Say again, where didst thou leave these varlets?

ARIEL. I told you, sir, they were red-hot with drinking;
So fun of valour that they smote the air
For breathing in their faces; beat the ground
For kissing of their feet; yet always bending
Towards their project. Then I beat my tabor;
At which, like unback'd colts, they prick'd their ears,
Advanced[287] their eyelids, lifted up their noses
As they smelt music: so I charm'd their ears
That calf-like they my lowing follow'd through
Tooth'd briers, sharp furzes, pricking gorse and thorns,
Which entered their frail shins: at last I left them
I' the filthy-mantled pool[288] beyond your cell,
There dancing up to the chins, that the foul lake
O'erstunk their feet.[289]

PROSPERO. This was well done, my bird.

---

285 "I thank ye" is addressed to Ferdinand and Miranda, in return for their "We wish you peace."

286 *To meet with* was anciently the same as to *counteract* or *oppose*. So in Herbert's *Country Parson*: "He knows the temper and pulse of every one in his house, and accordingly either *meets with* their vices, or advanceth their virtues."

287 *Advanced* is *raised*, as already explained. See page 37, note 110.—In the next line, "As they smelt," as *if* they smelt.

288 The pool mantled with filth. *Mantle* for the scum that forms on the surface of stagnant water. So in *The Merchant*, i. 1: "There are a sort of men whose visages do cream and *mantle* like a standing pond."

289 *That* for *so that* or *insomuch that*.—The meaning of this unsavoury passage is, that "the foul lake" was so stirred up by their dancing as to give out a worse odour than the men's feet did before they got into it.

Thy shape invisible retain thou still:
The trumpery in my house, go bring it hither,
For stale[290] to catch these thieves.

ARIEL. I go, I go. [*Exit.*]

PROSPERO. A devil, a born devil, on whose nature
Nurture can never stick;[291] on whom my pains,
Humanely taken, all, all lost, quite lost;
And as with age his body uglier grows,
So his mind cankers.[292] I will plague them all,
Even to roaring.—

[*Re-enter* ARIEL, *loaden with glistering apparel, &c.*]

Come, hang them on this line.[293]

[PROSPERO *and* ARIEL *remain invisible. Enter* CALIBAN, STEPHANO, *and* TRINCULO, *all wet.*]

CALIBAN. Pray you, tread softly, that the blind mole may not
Hear a foot fall: we now are near his cell.

STEPHANO. Monster, your fairy, which you say is a harmless fairy, has done little better than played the Jack with us.[294]

TRINCULO. Monster, I do smell all horse-piss; at which my nose is in great indignation.

---

[290] *Stale*, in the art of fowling, signified a *bait* or *lure* to decoy birds.

[291] *Nurture* for *education, training*, or *culture*.

[292] As before observed, page 37, note 112, *canker* was used of an eating, malignant sore, like *cancer*, which is but another form of the same word; and also of *rust.* I am not quite certain which of these senses it bears here; probably the first. Shakespeare has the word repeatedly in both senses; as in *Romeo and Juliet*, i. 1, where the first *canker'd* means *rusted*, while the second has the sense of *cancer*:

> To wield old partisans, in hands as old,
> *Canker'd* with peace, to part your *canker'd* hate.

[293] Some question has been made as to what *line* means here. The word is commonly taken as meaning a *clothes-line*; but I rather agree with the late Rev. Joseph Hunter, and with Mr. A. E. Brae, that it means a *line-tree*, which may well be supposed to be growing in the lawn before Prospero's cell,—the same that Stephano addresses a little after as "Mistress Line." For Prospero is still in the same place where he has just been making a display of his art; and I can hardly think he has a clothes-line stretched across it. It has indeed been objected that *line*, meaning the line-tree, would not be used thus, without the adjunct *tree* or *grove*; but Mr. Brae disposes of this objection fairly, by quoting the following from Holinshed: "We are not without the plane, the ugh, the sorfe, the chestnut, the *line*, the black cherrie, and such like."

[294] To play the *Jack* is to play the *Knave*; or it may be to play the *Jack-o'-lantern*, by leading them astray.

STEPHANO. So is mine.—Do you hear, monster? If I should take a displeasure against you, look you,—

TRINCULO. Thou wert but a lost monster.

CALIBAN. Good my lord,[295] give me thy favour still.
Be patient, for the prize I'll bring thee to
Shall hoodwink this mischance:[296] therefore speak softly.
All's hush'd as midnight yet.

TRINCULO. Ay, but to lose our bottles in the pool,—

STEPHANO. There is not only disgrace and dishonour in that, monster, but an infinite loss.

TRINCULO. That's more to me than my wetting: yet this is your harmless fairy, monster.

STEPHANO. I will fetch off my bottle, though I be o'er ears for my labour.

CALIBAN. Prithee, my king, be quiet. Seest thou here,
This is the mouth o' the cell: no noise, and enter.
Do that good mischief which may make this island
Thine own for ever, and I, thy Caliban,
For aye thy foot-licker.

STEPHANO. Give me thy hand. I do begin to have bloody thoughts.

TRINCULO. O King Stephano! O peer![297] O worthy Stephano! Look what a wardrobe here is for thee!

CALIBAN. Let it alone, thou fool; it is but trash.

TRINCULO. O, ho, monster! we know what belongs to a frippery.[298]— O King Stephano!

STEPHANO. Put off that gown, Trinculo; by this hand, I'll have that gown.

TRINCULO. Thy grace shall have it.

CALIBAN. The dropsy drown this fool I what do you mean
To dote thus on such luggage? Let's alone
And do the murder first: if he awake,
From toe to crown he'll fill our skins with pinches,

---

[295] We should say "my good lord." Similar inverted phrases occur continually in old plays; such as "dread my lord," "gracious my lord," "dear my mother," "sweet my sister," "gentle my brother," &c.

[296] To *hoodwink* a thing is, apparently, to make one *overlook* it or *forget* it, to *blind* him to it, or put it out of his sight. So *hoodman-blind* is an old term for what we call blind-man's buff.

[297] A humorous allusion to the old ballad entitled "Take thy old Cloak about thee," a part of which is sung by Iago in *Othello*, ii. 3. I add one stanza of it:

> *King Stephen* was a worthy *peer*,
> His breeches cost him but a crown;
> He held them sixpence all too dear,
> Therefore he call'd the tailor lown.

[298] *Frippery* was the name of a shop where old clothes were sold.

Make us strange stuff.

STEPHANO. Be you quiet, monster. Mistress line, is not this my jerkin? Now is the jerkin under the line: now, jerkin, you are like to lose your hair and prove a bald jerkin.[299]

[STEPHANO *and* TRINCULO *take garments.*]

TRINCULO. Do, do: we steal by line and level,[300] an't like your Grace.

STEPHANO. I thank thee for that jest; here's a garment for't: wit shall not go unrewarded while I am king of this country. *Steal by line and level* is an excellent pass of pate;[301] there's another garment for't.

TRINCULO. Monster, come, put some lime[302] upon your fingers, and away with the rest.

CALIBAN. I will have none on't: we shall lose our time,
And all be turn'd to barnacles,[303] or to apes
With foreheads villainous low.[304]

---

[299] King Stephano puns rather swiftly here. The name of the tree, as explained in note 293, suggests to him the *equinoctial line*, under which certain regions were much noted for their aptness to generate diseases that commonly made the sufferers *bald*, *Jerkin* was the name of a man's upper garment. Mr. Brae thinks there may be another quibble intended between *hair* and *air*, as clothes are hung out to be *aired*, and the jerkin was likely to lose the benefit of such *airing*; but I should rather take *hair* as referring to the *nap* of the jerkin, which was likely to be worn off in Stephano's using; so as to make the jerkin a *bald* jerkin in the nearer sense of having lost its *hair*.

[300] *Do, do*, is said, apparently, in commendation of Stephano's wit as displayed in his address to the jerkin.—"Steal by *line* and level" is a further punning on the same word; the plumb-line and the level being instruments used by architects and builders. So that to steal by line and level was to *show wit* in stealing, or to steal *artistically*.

[301] *Pass of pate* is a *spurt* or *sally of wit*; *pass* being, in the language of fencing, a *thrust*.

[302] *Lime*, or *bird-lime*, was a sticky substance used for catching birds. So in *2 Henry the Sixth*, i. 3: "Myself have *limed* a bush for her, and placed a quire of such enticing birds, that she will light to listen to their lays."

[303] Caliban's barnacle is the *clakis* or *tree-goose*, as it was called, which was thought to be produced from the shell-fish, *lepas antifera*, also called barnacle. Gerard's *Herbal* has the following account of the matter: "There are in the north parts of Scotland certain trees whereon do grow shell-fishes, which, falling into the water, do become fowls, whom we call *barnakles*, in the north of England *brant-geese*, and in Lancashire *tree-geese*." Perhaps the old notion of the barnacle-goose being produced by the barnacle-fish grew from the identity of name. As Caliban prides himself on his intellectuality, he naturally has a horror of being turned into any thing so stupid as a goose.

[304] A low forehead was held a deformity. On the other hand, a forehead high and broad was deemed a handsome feature in man or woman. The Poet has several allusions to this old idea. So in *The Two Gentlemen*, iv. 4: "Ay, but her forehead's low, and mine's as high." And in Spenser's description of Belphoebe, *Faerie Queene*, ii. 3, 24:

> Her ivorie forehead, full of bountie brave,
> Like a broad table did itselfe dispred.

STEPHANO. Monster, lay-to your fingers: help to bear this away where my hogshead of wine is, or I'll turn you out of my kingdom: go to,[305] carry this.
TRINCULO. And this.
STEPHANO. Ay, and this.

[*A noise of hunters heard. Enter divers Spirits, in shape of hounds, and hunt them about,* PROSPERO *and* ARIEL *setting them on.*]

PROSPERO. Hey, Mountain, hey!
ARIEL. Silver I there it goes, Silver!
PROSPERO. Fury, Fury! there, Tyrant, there! hark! hark!

[CALIBAN, STEPHANO, *and* TRINCULO, *are driven out.*]

[*To* ARIEL.] Go charge my goblins that they grind their joints
With dry convulsions;[306] shorten up their sinews
With aged cramps;[307] and more pinch-spotted make them
Than pard[308] or cat o' mountain.
ARIEL. Hark, they roar!
PROSPERO. Let them be hunted soundly. At this hour
Lie at my mercy all mine enemies:
Shortly shall all my labours end, and thou
Shalt have the air at freedom: for a little
Follow, and do me service. [*Exeunt.*]

---

[305] *Go to* is a phrase occurring very often, and of varying import, sometimes of impatience, sometimes of reproof, sometimes of encouragement. *Hush up, come on, be off* are among its meanings.

[306] In certain fevers, the mucilage sometimes gets dried out of the joints, especially the knee-joints, so as to cause a creaking or grating sound when the patient walks. Of course the effect is very painful.

[307] *Aged* seems to be used here with the sense of the intensive *old*, as before explained. See page 35, note 103.

[308] *Pard* was in common use for *leopard*, as also for *panther.—Cat-o'-mountain* is probably the *wild-cat.* So in Minsheu's *Spanish Dictionary*: "Gato montes: A cat of mountaine, a wilde cat." This animal, however, can hardly be called *spotted*; it is rather striped. Perhaps the term was not confined to one species of animal.

ACT V.

SCENE I.

Before the Cell of PROSPERO.

[*Enter* PROSPERO *in his magic robes, and* ARIEL.]

PROSPERO. Now does my project gather to a head:
My charms crack not; my spirits obey; and time
Goes upright with his carriage.[309] How's the day?
ARIEL. On the sixth hour; at which time, my lord,
You said our work should cease.
PROSPERO. I did say so,
When first I raised the tempest. Say, my spirit,
How fares the king and's followers?
ARIEL. Confined together
In the same fashion as you gave in charge,
Just as you left them; all prisoners, sir,
In the line-grove which weather-fends your cell;[310]
They cannot budge till your release.[311] The king,
His brother and yours, abide all three distracted
And the remainder mourning over them,
Brimful of sorrow and dismay; but chiefly
Him that you term'd, sir, *The good old lord Gonzalo*:
His tears run down his beard, like winter's drops
From eaves of reeds. Your charm so strongly works 'em
That if you now beheld them, your affections
Would become tender.
PROSPERO. Dost thou think so, spirit?
ARIEL. Mine would, sir, were I human.
PROSPERO. And mine shall.
Hast thou, which art but air, a touch, a feeling
Of their afflictions, and shall not myself,
One of their kind, that relish all as sharply,
Passion as they,[312] be kindlier moved than thou art?

---

[309] Time does not break down or bend under its load, or what it carries; that is, "we have time enough for what we have undertaken to do."

[310] "Which *defends* your cell against the weather, or the storm."

[311] "Till you release them," of course. The objective genitive, as it is called, where present usage admits only of the subjective genitive. The Poet has many such constructions. See page 70, note 251.

[312] *All* is here used adverbially, in the sense of *quite*; and *passion* is the object of *relish*, and has the sense of *suffering*. The sense of the passage is sometimes defeated by setting a comma after *sharply*.

Though with their high wrongs I am struck to the quick,
Yet with my nobler reason 'gainst my fury
Do I take part: the rarer action is
In virtue than in vengeance: they being penitent,
The sole drift of my purpose doth extend
Not a frown further. Go release them, Ariel:
My charms I'll break, their senses I'll restore,
And they shall be themselves.
ARIEL. I'll fetch them, sir. [*Exit.*]
PROSPERO. Ye elves of hills, brooks, standing lakes and groves;[313]
And ye that on the sands with printless foot
Do chase the ebbing Neptune and do fly him
When he comes back; you demi-puppets that
By moonshine do the green sour ringlets[314] make,
Whereof the ewe not bites, and you whose pastime
Is to make midnight mushrooms, that rejoice
To hear the solemn curfew;[315] by whose aid—
Weak masters though ye be[316]—I have bedimm'd
The noontide sun, call'd forth the mutinous winds,
And 'twixt the green sea and the azured vault
Set roaring war: to the dread rattling thunder
Have I given fire and rifted Jove's stout oak
With his own bolt; the strong-based promontory
Have I made shake and by the spurs[317] pluck'd up
The pine and cedar: graves at my command
Have waked their sleepers, oped, and let 'em forth
By my so potent art. But this rough magic
I here abjure, and, when I have required
Some heavenly music,—which even now I do,—
To work mine end upon their senses that
This airy charm is for, I'll break my staff,
Bury it certain fathoms in the earth,
And deeper than did ever plummet sound

---

313 This speech is in some measure borrowed from Medea's, in Ovid; the expressions are, many of them, in the old translation by Golding. But the exquisite fairy imagery is Shakespeare's own.

314 These *ringlets* were circles of bright-green grass, supposed to be produced by the footsteps of fairies dancing in a ring. The origin of them is still, I believe, a mystery. Alluded to in *A Midsummer-Night's Dream*, ii. 1.—*Mushrooms* were also thought to be the work of fairies; probably from their growing in rings, and springing up with such magical quickness.

315 They rejoice, because "the curfew tolls the knell of parting day," and so signals the time for the fairies to begin their nocturnal frolics.

316 *Weak*, if left to themselves, because they waste their force in sports and in frivolous or discordant aims; but powerful when guided by wisdom, and trained to worthy ends.

317 The *spurs* are the largest and the longest roots of trees.

I'll drown my book.—[*Solemn music.*]

[*Re-enter* ARIEL: *after him,* ALONSO, *with a frantic gesture, attended by* GONZALO; SEBASTIAN *and* ANTONIO *in like manner, attended by* ADRIAN *and* FRANCISCO *they all enter the circle which* PROSPERO *had made, and there stand charmed; which* PROSPERO *observing, speaks.*]

A solemn air and the best comforter
To an unsettled fancy cure thy brains,
Now useless, boil'd[318] within thy skull!—There stand,
For you are spell-stopp'd.—
Holy[319] Gonzalo, honourable man,
Mine eyes, even sociable to[320] the show of thine,
Fall fellowly drops.—The charm dissolves apace,
And as the morning steals upon the night,
Melting the darkness, so their rising senses[321]
Begin to chase the ignorant fumes that mantle
Their clearer reason.—O thou good Gonzalo,
My true preserver, and a loyal sir
To him you follow'st! I will pay thy graces
Home[322] both in word and deed.—Most cruelly
Didst thou, Alonso, use me and my daughter:
Thy brother was a furtherer in the act;—
Thou art pinch'd fort now, Sebastian.—Flesh and blood,
You, brother mine, that entertain'd ambition,
Expell'd remorse and nature;[323] who, with Sebastian,—

---

[318] *Boil'd* for boiling; the passive form with the *neuter* sense: for the verb to *boil* is used as active, passive, or neuter, indifferently. We have *boil'd* just so again in *The Winter's Tale*, iii. 3: "Would any but these *boil'd* brains of nineteen and two-and-twenty hunt this weather?"—Love, madness, and melancholy are imaged by Shakespeare under the figure of *boiled* brains, or *boiling* brains, or *seething* brains. So in *A Midsummer-Night's Dream*, v. 1: "Lovers and madmen have such *seething* brains," &c. Also in *Twelfth Night*, ii. 5: "If I lose a scruple of this sport, let me be *boiled* to death with melancholy." Probably the expression grew from the heat or fever that was understood or supposed to agitate the brain in such cases.

[319] In Shakespeare's time, *holy*, besides the religious sense of *godly* or *sanctified*, was also used in the moral sense of *righteous* or *just*.

[320] *Sociable to* is the same as *sympathetic with.*—*Fall*, in the next line, is evidently a transitive verb, equivalent to *let fall*. The usage was common. So in ii. 1, of this play: "To fall it on Gonzalo."

[321] *Senses* was very often used thus of the mental faculties; as we still say of one who does not see things as they are, that he is *out of his senses*. The meaning of the passage may be given something thus: "As morning dispels the darkness, so their returning reason begins to dispel the blinding mists or fumes that are gathered about it."

[322] *Home* was much used as a strong intensive; meaning *thoroughly*, or *to the utmost*.

Whose inward pinches therefore are most strong,
Would here have kill'd your king; I do forgive thee,
Unnatural though thou art.—Their understanding
Begins to swell, and the approaching tide
Will shortly fill the reasonable shore,[324]
That now lies foul and muddy. Not one of them
That yet looks on me, or would know me.—Ariel,
Fetch me the hat and rapier in my cell:—[*Exit* ARIEL.]
I will discase me,[325] and myself present
As I was sometime Milan:—quickly, spirit;
Thou shalt ere long be free.

[ARIEL *re-enters, singing, and helps to attire* PROSPERO.]

ARIEL. Where the bee sucks. there suck I:
In a cowslip's bell I lie;
There I couch when owls do cry.
On the bat's back I do fly
After summer merrily.[326]
Merrily, merrily shall I live now
Under the blossom that hangs on the bough.
PROSPERO. Why, that's my dainty Ariel! I shall miss thee:
But yet thou shalt have freedom: so, so, so.
To the king's ship, invisible as thou art:
There shalt thou find the mariners asleep
Under the hatches; the master and the boatswain
Being awake, enforce them to this place,
And presently, I prithee.
ARIEL. I drink the air before me, and return
Or ere your pulse twice beat. [*Exit.*]
GONZALO. All torment, trouble, wonder and amazement
Inhabits here: some heavenly power guide us
Out of this fearful country!
PROSPERO. Behold, sir king,
The wronged Duke of Milan, Prospero:

---

[323] Here, as commonly in Shakespeare, *remorse* is *pity* or *tenderness of* heart. *Nature* is put for *natural affection.* Often so.

[324] "The *reasonable* shore" is the shore *of reason.*

[325] "Will put off my disguise." The Poet repeatedly uses *case* for clothes; also for *skin.—Sometime*, in the next line, is *formerly.* Often so.

[326] Ariel uses "the bat's back" as his vehicle, to pursue Summer in its progress to other regions, and thus live under continual blossoms. Such appears the most natural as well as most poetical meaning of this much-disputed passage. In fact, however, bats do not migrate in quest of Summer, but become torpid in Winter. Was the Poet ignorant of this, or did he disregard it, thinking that such beings as Ariel were not bound to observe the rules of natural history?

For more assurance that a living prince
Does now speak to thee, I embrace thy body;
And to thee and thy company I bid
A hearty welcome.

ALONSO. Whêr[327] thou best he or no,
Or some enchanted trifle[328] to abuse me,
As late I have been, I not know: thy pulse
Beats as of flesh and blood; and, since I saw thee,
The affliction of my mind amends, with which,
I fear, a madness held me: this must crave,
An if this be at all[329]—a most strange story.
Thy dukedom I resign,[330] and do entreat
Thou pardon me my wrongs.[331] But how should Prospero
Be living and be here?

PROSPERO. [*To* GONZALO.] First, noble friend,
Let me embrace thine age, whose honour cannot
Be measured or confined.

GONZALO. Whether this be
Or be not, I'll not swear.

PROSPERO. You do yet taste
Some subtlities[332] o' the isle, that will not let you
Believe things certain. Welcome, my friends all!
[*Aside to* SEBASTIAN *and* ANTONIO.] But you, my brace of lords, were I so minded,
I here could pluck his highness' frown upon you
And justify you traitors:[333] at this time
I will tell no tales.

SEBASTIAN. [*Aside to* ANTONIO.] The Devil speaks in him.

PROSPERO. Now,

---

[327] The Poet often so contracts *whether*.

[328] *Enchanted trifle* probably means *bewitching phantom. Enchanted* for *enchanting*, in accordance with the usage, before noted, of active and passive forms indiscriminately. See page 30, note 76. Walker, however, thinks the meaning to be "some trifle *produced by enchantment* to abuse me."—*Abuse* was often used in the sense of *deceive*, *delude*, or *cheat*.

[329] That is, if there be any reality in all this. *An if*, again, as before explained. See page 55, note 195.

[330] The dukedom of Milan had been made tributary to Naples by Antonio, as the price of aid in his usurpation.

[331] Still another instance of the construction mentioned in note 311 of this scene. "*My* wrongs" may mean either the wrongs I have *done*, or the wrongs I have *suffered*. Here it means the former.

[332] *Subtilties* are quaint deceptive inventions; the word is common to ancient cookery, in which a disguised or ornamented dish is so termed. Fabyan's *Chronicle*, 1542, describes one made of pastry," called a pelican sitting on his nest with his birds, and an image of Saint Catharine holding a book, and disputing with the doctors."

[333] "*Prove* you traitors," or, "justify myself for calling you such."

For you, most wicked sir, whom to call brother
Would even infect my mouth, I do forgive
Thy rankest fault; all of them; and require
My dukedom of thee, which perforce,[334] I know,
Thou must restore.
ALONSO. If thou be'st Prospero,
Give us particulars of thy preservation;
How thou hast met us here, who three hours since
Were wreck'd upon this shore; where I have lost—
How sharp the point of this remembrance is!—
My dear son Ferdinand.
PROSPERO. I'm woe[335] for't, sir.
ALONSO. Irreparable is the loss, and patience
Says it is past her cure.
PROSPERO. I rather think
You have not sought her help, of whose soft grace
For the like loss I have her sovereign aid
And rest myself content.
ALONSO. You the like loss!
PROSPERO. As great to me as late;[336] and, supportable
To make the dear loss, have I means much weaker
Than you may call to comfort you, for I
Have lost my daughter.
ALONSO. A daughter?
O heavens, that they were living both in Naples,
The king and queen there! that they were, I wish
Myself were mudded in that oozy bed
Where my son lies. When did you lose your daughter?
PROSPERO. In this last tempest. I perceive these lords
At this encounter do so much admire,[337]
That they devour their reason and scarce think
Their eyes do offices of truth, their words
Are natural breath:[338] but, howsoe'er you have
Been jostled from your senses, know for certain
That I am Prospero and that very duke
Which was thrust forth of Milan, who most strangely
Upon this shore, where you were wreck'd, was landed,

---

[334] *Perforce* is *of force*, that is, necessarily or of necessity.

[335] *Woe* was often used thus with an adjective sense; sorry.

[336] "As great to me, *and* as *recent*." Or the meaning may be, "As great to me as *it is* recent." Either explanation suits, but I prefer the first.—*Portable* is *endurable*. The Poet has it repeatedly.

[337] Shakespeare commonly uses *admire* and its derivatives in the Latin sense; that of *wonder* or *amazement*. The meaning here is, that their reason is swallowed up in wonder.

[338] "That the words I am speaking are those of a real living man."

To be the lord on't. No more yet of this;[339]
For 'tis a chronicle of day by day,
Not a relation for a breakfast nor
Befitting this first meeting. Welcome, sir;
This cell's my court: here have I few attendants
And subjects none abroad: pray you, look in.
My dukedom since you have given me again,
I will requite you with as good a thing;
At least bring forth a wonder, to content ye
As much as me my dukedom.

[*The entrance of the Cell opens, and discovers* FERDINAND *and* MIRANDA *playing at chess*.]

MIRANDA. Sweet lord, you play me false.
FERDINAND. No, my dear'st love,
I would not for the world.
MIRANDA. Yes, for a score of kingdoms you should wrangle,[340]
And I would call it, fair play.
ALONSO. If this prove
A vision of the Island, one dear son
Shall I twice lose.[341]
SEBASTIAN. A most high miracle!
FERDINAND. Though the seas threaten, they are merciful;
I have cursed them without cause. [*Kneels to* ALONSO.]
ALONSO. Now all the blessings
Of a glad father compass thee about!
Arise, and say how thou camest here.
MIRANDA. O, wonder!
How many goodly creatures are there here!
How beauteous mankind is! O brave new world,
That has such people in't!
PROSPERO. 'Tis new to thee.

---

[339] No more of this *now*, or *for the present.* So *yet* was often used.

[340] The sense evidently wanted here is, "you *might play me false*"; but how to get this out of wrangle, is not very apparent. Was *wrangle* used as a technical term in chess and other games? In *King Henry V.*, i. 2, we have this: "He hath made a match with such a *wrangler*, that all the Courts of France will be disturb'd with chases." This is said with reference to the game of tennis; and *wrangler* here seems to mean *opponent* or *antagonist. Wrangle*, however, is from the same original as *wrong*, and its radical sense is the same. Mr. Joseph Crosby thinks the word is used here in this its radical sense. He writes me as follows: "In the North of England, *wrangdom* is a common word for *wrong*, and *wrangously* for *wrongfully. Wrangle* in this sentence is an explanatory parallelism of Miranda's 'play me false,' and means *wrong me*,—cheat me in the game."

[341] "Shall *twice* lose" appears to mean "shall lose a *second time.*" He has in effect lost his son once in supposing him drowned; and will lose him again in the dispelling of the vision, if vision it should prove.

ALONSO. What is this maid with whom thou wast at play?
Your eld'st acquaintance cannot be three hours:
Is she the goddess that hath sever'd us,
And brought us thus together?
FERDINAND. Sir, she is mortal;
But by immortal Providence she's mine:
I chose her when I could not ask my father
For his advice, nor thought I had one. She
Is daughter to this famous Duke of Milan,
Of whom so often I have heard renown,
But never saw before; of whom I have
Received a second life; and second father
This lady makes him to me.
ALONSO. I am hers:
But, O, how oddly will it sound that I
Must ask my child forgiveness!
PROSPERO. There, sir, stop:
Let us not burthen our remembrance with
A heaviness that's gone.
GONZALO. I have inly wept,
Or should have spoke ere this. Look down, you god,
And on this couple drop a blessed crown!
For it is you that have chalk'd forth the way
Which brought us hither.
ALONSO. I say, Amen, Gonzalo!
GONZALO. Was Milan thrust from Milan, that his issue
Should become kings of Naples? O, rejoice
Beyond a common joy, and set it down
With gold on lasting pillars: In one voyage
Did Claribel her husband find at Tunis,
And Ferdinand, her brother, found a wife
Where he himself was lost, Prospero his dukedom
In a poor isle and all of us ourselves
When no man was his own.[342]
ALONSO. [*To* FERDINAND and MIRANDA] Give me your hands:
Let grief and sorrow still embrace his heart
That doth not wish you joy!
GONZALO. Be't so! Amen!—

[*Re-enter* ARIEL, *with the* MASTER *and* BOATSWAIN *amazedly following.*]

O, look, sir, look, sir! here is more of us:

---

[342] When no man was *in his senses*, or had self-possession.

I prophesied, if a gallows were on land,
This fellow could not drown.—Now, blasphemy,
That swear'st grace o'erboard, not an oath on shore?
Hast thou no mouth by land? What is the news?
BOATSWAIN. The best news is, that we have safely found
Our king and company; the next, our ship—
Which, but three glasses since, we gave out split—
Is tight and yare and bravely rigg'd as when
We first put out to sea.
ARIEL. [*Aside to* PROSPERO.] Sir, all this service
Have I done since I went.
PROSPERO. [*Aside to* ARIEL.] My tricksy[343] spirit!
ALONSO. These are not natural events; they strengthen
From strange to stranger.—Say, how came you hither?
BOATSWAIN. If I did think, sir, I were well awake,
I'd strive to tell you. We were dead of sleep,
And—how we know not—all clapp'd under hatches;
Where but even now with strange and several noises
Of roaring, shrieking, howling, jingling chains,
And more diversity of sounds, all horrible,
We were awaked; straightway, at liberty;
Where we, in all her trim, freshly beheld
Our royal, good and gallant ship, our master
Capering to eye her:[344] on a trice, so please you,
Even in a dream, were we divided from them
And were brought moping[345] hither.
ARIEL. [*Aside to* PROSPERO.] Was't well done?
PROSPERO. [*Aside to* ARIEL.] Bravely, my diligence. Thou shalt be free.
ALONSO. This is as strange a maze as e'er men trod
And there is in this business more than nature
Was ever conduct of:[346] some oracle
Must rectify our knowledge.
PROSPERO. Sir, my liege,
Do not infest your mind with beating on[347]
The strangeness of this business; at pick'd leisure
Which shall be shortly, single I'll resolve[348] you—

---

[343] Ariel seems to be called *tricksy*, because his execution has the celerity of magic, or of a juggler's tricks: "clever, adroit, dexterous," says Dyce.

[344] "Capering *to eye* her" is leaping or dancing with joy *at seeing* her. Still another instance of the infinitive used gerundively.

[345] To *mope* is to be *dull* or *stupid*; originally, *dim-sighted.*

[346] *Conduct* for *conductor*; that is, *guide* or *leader.* Often so.

[347] We have a like expression in use now,—"Still hammering at it."

[348] In Shakespeare, to *resolve* often means to *satisfy*, or to *explain satisfactorily.*—*Single* appears to be used adverbially here, its force going with the predicate; and the last

Which to you shall seem probable—of every
These happen'd accidents; till when, be cheerful
And think of each thing well.—[*Aside to* ARIEL.] Come hither, spirit:
Set Caliban and his companions free;
Untie the spell. [*Exit* ARIEL.]—How fares my gracious sir?
There are yet missing of your company
Some few odd lads that you remember not.

[*Re-enter* ARIEL, *driving in* CALIBAN, STEPHANO *and* TRINCULO, *in their stolen apparel.*]

STEPHANO. Every man shift for all the rest,[349] and let no man take care for himself; for all is but fortune. Coragio, bully-monster, coragio!

TRINCULO. If these be true spies which I wear in my head, here's a goodly sight.

CALIBAN. O Setebos, these be brave spirits indeed!
How fine my master is! I am afraid
He will chastise me.

SEBASTIAN. Ha, ha!
What things are these, my lord Antonio?
Will money buy 'em?

ANTONIO. Very like; one of them
Is a plain fish, and, no doubt, marketable.

PROSPERO. Mark but the badges of these men, my lords,
Then say if they be true. This misshapen knave,
His mother was a witch, and one so strong
That could control the moon, make flows and ebbs,
And deal in her command without her power.[350]
These three have robb'd me; and this demi-devil—
For he's a bastard one—had plotted with them
To take my life. Two of these fellows you
Must know and own; this thing of darkness!
Acknowledge mine.

CALIBAN. I shall be pinch'd to death.

---

which refers to *resolve*: "I will explain to you—and the explanation shall seem to you natural and likely—all these incidents, *severally*, or *in detail*, as they have happened."—CROSBY.

349 Stephano's tongue is rather tipsy still, and staggers into a misplacement of his words. He means "Let every man shift for himself."

350 *Without* has here the sense of *beyond*; a common usage in the Poet's time. So in *A Midsummer-Night's Dream*, iv. 1: "Where we might be *without* the peril of th' Athenian law." And in Jonson's Cynthia'*s Revels*, i. 4: "O, now I apprehend you: your phrase was without me before." So that the meaning of the text is, "who could outdo the Moon in exercising the Moon in exercising the Moon's own command."

ALONSO. Is not this Stephano, my drunken butler?
SEBASTIAN. He is drunk now: where had he wine?
ALONSO. And Trinculo is reeling ripe: where should they
Find this grand liquor that hath gilded[351] 'em?
[*To* TRINCULO.] How camest thou in this pickle?
TRINCULO. I have been in such a pickle since I saw you last that, I fear me, will never out of my bones: I shall not fear fly-blowing.[352]
SEBASTIAN. Why, how now, Stephano!
STEPHANO. O, touch me not; I am not Stephano, but a cramp.
PROSPERO. You'd be king o' the isle, sirrah?
STEPHANO. I should have been a sore one,[353] then.
ALONSO. [*Pointing to* CALIBAN.] This is a strange thing as e'er I look'd on.
PROSPERO. He is as disproportion'd in his manners
As in his shape.—Go, sirrah, to my cell;
Take with you your companions; as you look
To have my pardon, trim it handsomely.
CALIBAN. Ay, that I will; and I'll be wise hereafter
And seek for grace. What a thrice-double ass
Was I, to take this drunkard for a god
And worship this dull fool!
PROSPERO. Go to; away!
ALONSO. Hence, and bestow your luggage where you found it.
SEBASTIAN. Or stole it, rather. [*Exeunt* CALIBAN, STEPHANO, *and* TRINCULO.]
PROSPERO. [*to* ALONSO.] Sir, I invite your highness and your train
To my poor cell, where you shall take your rest
For this one night; which, part of it, I'll waste
With such discourse as, I not doubt, shall make it
Go quick away; the story of my life
And the particular accidents gone by
Since I came to this isle: and in the morn
I'll bring you to your ship and so to Naples,

---

[351] The phrase *being gilded* was a trite one for *being drunk*; perhaps because drinking puts one into *golden altitudes.* It has been suggested, also, that there is an allusion to the *grand elixir* of the alchemists, which was an ideal medicine for *gilding* a base metal in the sense of *transmuting it into gold*; as also for repairing health in man. This, too, is probable; for the Poet is fond of clustering various ideas round a single image.

[352] Trinculo is playing rather deeply upon *pickle*; and one of the senses here intended is that of being pickled in salt or brine so as not to become tainted. *Fly-blows* are the maggot-eggs deposited by flies; and to fly-blow is to taint with such eggs.

[353] A pun upon the different senses of *sore*, one of which is harsh, *severe*, or *oppressive.* The same equivoque occurs in *2 Henry the Sixth*, iv. 7, where Dick proposes that Cade's mouth be the source of English law, and John remarks, aside,—"Mass, 'twill be a *sore* law, then; for he was thrust in the mouth with a spear, and 'tis not whole yet."

Where I have hope to see the nuptial
Of these our dear-beloved solemnized;
And thence retire me[354] to my Milan, where
Every third thought shall be my grave.
ALONSO. I long
To hear the story of your life, which must
Take the ear strangely.
PROSPERO. I'll deliver all;
And promise you calm seas, auspicious gales
And sail so expeditious that shall catch
Your royal fleet far off.—[*Aside to* ARIEL.] My Ariel, chick,
That is thy charge: then to the elements
Be free, and fare thou well!—Please you, draw near.

[*Exeunt.*]

---

354 That is, *withdraw myself.* The Poet has various instances of *retire* thus used as a transitive verb.

Epilogue

PROSPERO.

Now my charms are all o'erthrown,
And what strength I have's mine own,
Which is most faint: now, 'tis true,
I must be here confined by you,
Or sent to Naples. Let me not,
Since I have my dukedom got
And pardon'd the deceiver, dwell
In this bare island by your spell;
But release me from my bands
With the help of your good hands.[1]
Gentle breath of yours my sails
Must fill, or else my project fails,
Which was to please. Now I want
Spirits to enforce, art to enchant,
And my ending is despair,
Unless I be relieved by prayer,
Which pierces so that it assaults
Mercy itself and frees all faults.
As you from crimes would pardon'd be,
Let your indulgence set me free.

THE END

---

[1] The Epilogue is supposed to be addressed to the theatrical audience, and the speaker here solicits their applause by the clapping of their hands. Noise was a breaker of enchantments and spells; hence the applause would release him from his bonds.

Made in the USA
Lexington, KY
09 April 2019